An Extraordinary School

Re-modelling special education

Edited by Sara James

ACER Press

KH

First published 2012
by ACER Press, an imprint of
Australian Council for Educational Research Ltd
19 Prospect Hill Road, Camberwell Victoria, 3124, Australia

www.acerpress.com.au
sales@acer.edu.au

Note: This book was written over several years. Some of the identities,
diagnoses and stories of the students, parents and staff members in this book
have been combined or altered to protect the privacy of students or to present
examples that represent the general experience of staff, students or parents.

Excerpt on p. xii from 'From Little Things Big Things Grow', written and composed by Paul
Kelly and Kev Carmody, published by Sony/ATV Music Publishing Australia.

Edited by Rebecca Leech
Cover design, text design and typesetting by ACER Project Publishing
Cover photograph by Anna Pawloski
Images in the colour section © Port Phillip Specialist School, used with permission. With
thanks to the photographers: Anita Bragge, Dan Dinnen, Chris Edmonds, Clare Duncan,
Anne Schwartz, Yvonne Miller, Alison Druce and Tony Spiker.
Printed in Australia by BPA Print Group

National Library of Australia Cataloguing-in-Publication entry:

Title:	An extraordinary school : re-modelling special education/ edited by Sara James
ISBN:	9781742860121 (pbk.)
Notes:	Includes bibliographical references.
Subjects:	Port Phillip Specialist School (Vic). Special education—Victoria. Children with disabilities—Education—Victoria.
Other Authors/Contributors:	James, Sara.
Dewey Number:	371.909945

MIX
Paper from
responsible sources
FSC® C015950
www.fsc.org

11/12/13

For Sophie
and all siblings of children with special needs.
In celebration of who they are.

When you first meet a child with a disability,
you see all the things they can't do.
And then when you know them,
you see all the things they can do.

Foreword

You are about to enter a new world. A world that is not what it seems. A world that *is* special. It is a place where problems are faced with myriad fascinating, brilliant and creative solutions. You are about to enter the world of Port Phillip Specialist School.

Port Phillip Specialist School has re-thought how special education is taught. Its three-pronged approach to education involving a full-service school model, an arts-based curriculum and integrated service delivery *is* modern education.

One of the great joys of this book is seeing art at the coalface. Art isn't merely decoration, fun or a distraction. At Port Phillip Specialist School, art is a verb as well as a noun. Art is a language, it is a solution. It is through art, music, drama and dance that the team at Port Phillip Specialist School help students to achieve their full potential both in educational terms and in life skills, even when these skills are things that most of us would take for granted.

Having worked in the arts for my entire professional life, I know you're only as good as your band. Port Phillip Specialist School understands this. Its integrated team of teachers, therapists and staff carry out their work with courage, patience and humour and their dedication shows in the outcomes their students attain.

Unlike Shakespeare's 'whining schoolboy ... creeping like a snail unwillingly to school', one of my favourite stories in this book involves a student who runs five kilometres to Port Phillip Specialist School. RUNS. Reflect on that.

This school's vision is breathtaking in its scope and clarity. It should be at the forefront of educational thinking for all schools.

Dear reader, you are about to understand what it is to stand on the shoulders of giants. Really. Enjoy.

Rhys Muldoon

Contents

About the editor

. . . .

Sara James is an award-winning foreign correspondent and author. As a New York–based correspondent for *Dateline NBC*, James criss-crossed the globe to report on many of the watershed events of our era. James also served as a frequent substitute anchor on the news desk of NBC News' *Today*. Her first book, *The Best of Friends: Two Women, Two Continents, and One Enduring Friendship*, co-authored with Ginger Mauney, was published by HarperCollins in 2007. In 2008, James moved from New York City to the Melbourne area with her Australian husband Andrew Butcher and their daughters, Sophie and Jacqueline. James now covers Australasia for NBC. She used her reporting skills to investigate special education in Victoria, Australia, and was delighted to discover the innovative program at Port Phillip Specialist School. Jacqueline attends Port Phillip Specialist School.

About the contributors

Anita Bragge trained in fine art printmaking following a degree in cultural studies. She worked and studied as an artist before training in art therapy. She has also worked as a freelance arts writer. She currently works as an art therapist at Port Phillip Specialist School (PPSS) in Melbourne.

Professor Brian J. Caldwell is Managing Director and Principal Consultant at Educational Transformations in Australia and Associate Director of the Schools Network in England. From 1998 to 2004 he served as Dean of Education at the University of Melbourne where he is currently Professorial Fellow. His international work over the last 25 years includes more than 500 presentations, projects and other professional assignments in or for 40 countries. His most recent books are *Why Not the Best Schools?* (2008) with Jessica Harris, *Our School Our Future* (2010) with David Loader, *Changing Schools in an Era of Globalization* (2011) with John Chi-Kin Lee and *Transforming Education through the Arts* (2012) with Tanya Vaughan.

Emeritus Professor Martin Comte OAM is an Honorary Life Member and Fellow of the Australian Society for Music Education, and a Fellow of the Australian College of Educators. He was appointed to the first Australian-university Chair in Music Education, at RMIT University in 1993.

Dan Dinnen has worked extensively in the arts as a performer and an educator, completing his postgraduate Diploma of Education (Secondary Drama and English) at the University of Sydney in 1995. After a long and satisfying chapter running workshops and programs at some of Australia's most renowned youth theatre companies, Dan sought a change of direction and found it in his current position as drama teacher at PPSS. As well as his work at PPSS, Dan is a working musician who sings and plays guitar and harmonica, performing both as a solo artist and with several Melbourne-based blues music groups.

Dr Carl Parsons initially trained as a speech–language pathologist and audiologist. He also completed a Master's degree in Education and a PhD in Communication Disorders and Psychology. Much of his work has been with children. Carl worked at the Lincoln Institute/Lincoln School of Health Sciences at LaTrobe University from 1980 to 1999 where he was the Associate Professor of Childhood Language Disorders, Associate Dean for Research, Chairperson in the School of Human Communication Disorders, Head of Podiatry, and Deputy Dean of the Faculty of Health Sciences. Carl is a patron and life member of the Down Syndrome Association of Victoria. He is known for his multidisciplinary work and his communication camps that have been run in every state and territory of Australia. He has published more than 100 articles on communication disorders in international refereed journals. In 1999, he joined the staff at PPSS as Director of Integrated Services. He is also the National Coordinator of Programs for Shine, a division of the Andrew Dean Fildes Foundation that assists children with language-learning disabilities.

Tony Spiker has been playing drums and percussion since he was seven, and left school at age 16 to play in bands. He spent nine years in London pursuing his career as a session musician and travelled frequently to Rio de Janeiro to explore his interest in Brazilian percussion. Tony is married with three children, and first came to PPSS as a parent, as his daughter who has autism was enrolled as a student. He made a significant presentation at the International Symposium on Re-imagining Special Education through Arts Education and Arts Therapy (RiSE Symposium) about his work at PPSS.

Bronwyn Welch initially trained as a music therapist and worked for 10 years in special education and early intervention before retraining as a special education teacher. In 2007, she travelled to Paris, England and Singapore to learn more about how different services for people with disabilities incorporated the arts into their programs. Bronwyn is currently working part-time while her child is young.

Introduction

∙∙

'From little things, big things grow.'
Paul Kelly and Kev Carmody

To walk into Port Phillip Specialist School (PPSS) is to embark on an amazing journey. The school radiates energy, optimism and creativity. Visitors invariably remark upon how engaged the children seem to be in their learning. Nestled near Melbourne's Port Phillip Bay, this remarkable school has become a kind of educational lighthouse—a beacon of hope and possibility, and a leader in the field of special education.

What makes PPSS so different? The school uses a unique, tripartite approach to teach children with intellectual and physical disabilities: it is a 'fully-serviced' facility; employs an integrated services approach to teaching; and offers an arts-based curriculum. The school's innovative program is attracting interest internationally, and education experts from the United States, the United Kingdom, Germany and Singapore have flown to Australia to study PPSS. In addition, recent neurological research also supports the school's methods (as explained in detail in Chapter 8).

This is the story of PPSS and its original brand of special education. *An Extraordinary School* explores the theoretical underpinnings of the school, demonstrates how theory is put into practice in the classroom and provides first-hand accounts from a number of teachers and specialists.

It is impossible to tell the story of PPSS without also telling the story of Bella Irlicht, the principal of PPSS from 1988 to 2008. Bella grew the school from 19 students and six teachers holding classes in a small house to 150 students and a diverse staff of 65 practitioners and administrators situated in a large complex.

The Victorian state government first started providing special education in the 1970s, either in separate special schools or within mainstream classrooms. Prior to that, most children with intellectual disabilities were taught at home or were housed in institutions. There was no structured curriculum for special education; nor were the children expected to reach any particular targets or milestones. Bella says the accepted wisdom was that it was enough to keep the students occupied and teach them the most rudimentary skills.

Slowly, special education began to change and improve, and Bella was at the vanguard. She believed children with intellectual disabilities had genuine potential to learn. The question was: How best to unlock that potential? During her 20-year tenure, Bella provided crucial vision and leadership, and her skills as a fundraiser helped this public school acquire the state-of-the-art facilities and specialised equipment she believed essential to teach children with additional needs. Those facilities include three playgrounds, a heated indoor pool, a stand-alone house where students practise independent living skills and a multimillion dollar performing arts centre. Bella knew that having a skilled team and providing the school with ample resources were only the first steps. She believed it also was crucial to change how special education was taught. During her tenure at PPSS she brought about three major innovations: turning PPSS into a fully-serviced school, creating an integrated services curriculum and committee, and developing an arts-based curriculum.

A fully-serviced school

The first of her three major innovations—to turn PPSS into a fully-serviced school—was born of Bella's belief that a school should respond to the myriad requirements of each child, rather than simply address his or her performance in the classroom. Bella was convinced the best way to meet the needs of children with intellectual disabilities was to have various specialists available under one roof, and began implementing a more holistic program at PPSS beginning in 1994. She then discovered that similar ideas were being explored simultaneously in the US in relation to inner-city children from disadvantaged backgrounds. As Joy Dryfoos explains in her book *Full-Service Schools*, such a facility:

> ... integrates education, medical, social and/or human services that are beneficial to meeting the needs of children and youth and their families on school grounds or in locations which are easily accessible.

> A full-service school provides the types of prevention, treatment, and support services children and families need to succeed. (Florida legislation, cited in Dryfoos 1994, p. 142)

In 1995, Bella was awarded a Churchill Fellowship to study how several American schools were implementing the concept. Based on that research, she adopted for PPSS Dryfoos' title of fully-serviced school and revised and enhanced the program at the school. In her research on fully-serviced schools and students with disabilities, author Cynthia Warger (2001) noted that 'integrating services at the school holds particular promise for improving outcomes for these children'. Under the full-service model, PPSS employs a range of special education teachers, therapists, paramedical staff, specialists in the arts, psychologists, social workers and other relevant professionals, who all work on-site.

Integrated services

Bella also realised it was imperative for members of PPSS's wide-ranging faculty to collaborate in order to achieve the best results for students. That led to the school's second major innovation: creating an integrated services curriculum overseen by an Integrated Services Committee. The approach ensured that relatively scarce resources, such as physiotherapy, occupational therapy and speech therapy, were made more available to students by weaving these therapies throughout the entire school day. At PPSS, therapists not only conduct one-on-one sessions with individual children; they also train classroom teachers, assistants and various arts specialists to deliver specific, individualised therapies for each child within the context of a variety of other lessons. Expertise is spread more widely, the children receive more therapy and the funding goes further.

The Integrated Services Committee convenes twice a week to discuss the needs of individual children at the school. The team pays particular attention to each student's educational goals, but also considers any medical concerns, social issues, difficulties at home or other relevant information that could affect a child's success at school. Comprised of representatives from various specialties at the school, the committee's task is to make sure every student achieves his or her greatest potential. The committee is considered central to the success of PPSS.

Full service and integrated services are more than just concepts; they are both fundamental to PPSS and are examples of how the school continues to innovate, refine and improve special education. Underlying the various approaches employed at the school is a desire to discover the best way to teach children. Children such as, for example, a seven-year-old boy we'll call Jacob. Jacob has significant motor and sensory difficulties, as well as an intellectual disability. Suffering such poor balance that he was unable to walk, Jacob would sometimes lie on the floor of his classroom, banging his head, spitting, even gagging. His classroom teacher used a variety of strategies to try to increase Jacob's mobility and relieve his frustration, as did the school's physiotherapists, yet Jacob could not walk unassisted. How could the school better help Jacob?

As a fully-serviced school, PPSS employs a full-time swimming instructor, who noticed that Jacob seemed calm, relaxed and confident in the pool. Jacob's smiles and laughter gave clear evidence of his delight. Observing Jacob and other equally enthusiastic children led to the school's swimming instructor and occupational therapist attending a specialised seminar to study the latest techniques in hydrotherapy. The school's swimming instructor Anna Pawloski noted, 'Using the water to support students with physical disabilities, we have been able to maintain or increase the range of movement of their muscles, their stamina for physical activity and their overall strength.' Based on this, PPSS instituted a new program targeting Jacob, among other students, during 2010. As we explore later, there were tangible, positive results. Anna stated, 'Our greatest success in the hydrotherapy program this year was two students independently walking up to 20 metres in the water.'

An arts-based curriculum

PPSS's third innovation was the development and introduction of an arts-based curriculum. Bella's experience at PPSS convinced her that the conventional way of teaching children within special education simply wasn't effective. She believed these children learned more slowly than their mainstream peers and also learned in different ways. Yet they were expected to follow, to the best of their ability, the same curriculum used by students who did not have special learning needs.

PPSS offers a range of music, dance, drama and art classes, as well as music, art and drama therapy. Bella noticed that students seemed especially engaged in their learning when they were participating in the arts. She wondered if the arts might hold the key to helping children with intellectual disabilities. Bella approached education consultant Pam Russell to assist with the development of the curriculum. Pam put together a team of people who had strengths and expertise in various areas, and who listened to teachers, therapists and parents of students at the school and then designed a blueprint for a new kind of education. Students across the state of Victoria have followed the Victorian Essential Learning Standards since 2005; PPSS unveiled its Visual and Performing Arts Curriculum, or VPAC, the same year. Although it is rare for a school to create its own curriculum, Bella says because the VPAC was embedded in sound theory and practice, and the conceptual framework fitted within the state guidelines, it was readily accepted by the Victorian education department.

VPAC isn't a program to teach the arts, but a vehicle to deliver a curriculum through the arts. Put another way, PPSS isn't training students to be dancers, musicians, artists or actors; rather, the school employs dance, music, art and drama to teach children communication, numeracy and living skills. While there are other schools teaching special education that use the arts, no-one else offers an arts-based curriculum quite like VPAC.

But should similar programs be instituted elsewhere? Should children with intellectual disabilities be taught using an arts-based curriculum? Is there proof that teaching through the arts is a superior strategy and should be replicated?

Monitoring student progress

Offering 'proof' is challenging when it comes to charting the progress of children with intellectual disabilities. Standardised tests like Australia's National Assessment Program—Literacy and Numeracy (NAPLAN) are unhelpful, as those tests are developed to assess a range of children without learning needs whose scores fall along a bell curve. But children with an IQ of 69 or below—the requirement to attend a specialist school such as PPSS—are not on that curve.

Furthermore, children with intellectual disabilities are highly individual and idiosyncratic. Children at PPSS might have Down syndrome,

Angelman syndrome, could be on the autism spectrum or could have suffered a stroke at birth. Even children with the same disability often present quite differently. While PPSS conducts standardised tests to assess student performance, those at the school believe the best way to assess how a given child is faring is to compare that child to himself or herself over the course of a year. Has there been progress, regression or a plateau?

PPSS documents changes in its students with photographs and videos and through a specially designed computer program. Each day, every teacher records the skills attempted with a student (such as counting to five), which modality has been used (such as art, physical education or music), and whether the student performed that skill at a low, medium or high level (whether the child jumped five times or stacked five blocks). Those results are tracked through the computer program, so that the school can monitor what each teacher is doing, what each student is achieving and which methods work best for each individual student.

The school is currently creating a new program to analyse classroom data to provide quantitative evidence of how its approach is working overall. Until then, the best evidence that the school's arts-based curriculum is the right approach is linked to research into how the brain functions. Psychiatrist Norman Doidge (2007) offers evidence that the brain is not 'fixed' or 'hard-wired', as previously thought, but is capable of profound change throughout our lives. This neuroplasticity—the ability of the brain to construct new pathways around cognitive roadblocks—has crucial implications for special education. Doidge notes, 'children are not always stuck with the mental abilities they are born with ... the damaged brain can often reorganize itself so that when one part fails, another can often substitute' (p. xv).

So, how best to foster neuroplasticity? If educators can discover ways to increase and enhance this change, children with an intellectual disability may be able to learn more. The arts, particularly music, are potent tools for achieving change. Oliver Sacks explores what he considers the musical instinct of the human species. Sacks writes:

> ... while music can affect all of us—calm us, animate us, comfort us, thrill us, or serve to organize and synchronize us at work or play— it may be especially powerful and have great therapeutic potential for patients with a variety of neurological conditions ... Some are retarded, some autistic; others have subcortical syndromes ... All of these

conditions and many others can potentially respond to music and music therapy. (2007, p. xiii)

Consider the case of Jared, who has profound autism, is non-verbal, has significant behaviour issues and started at PPSS from Prep. He was prone to severe tantrums whenever he was overstimulated, which happened frequently, as he was hypersensitive to auditory and visual stimuli. He also had challenging and even repellent behaviours. Jared hit other students and staff, smeared faeces and even tried to sniff the bottoms of other students as they walked by.

Jared was 13 when PPSS adopted the VPAC curriculum in 2005. As time passed, teachers and specialists began to notice subtle changes in Jared. Music seemed to calm and soothe him. Although he still had tantrums, they were less frequent, less violent and shorter. While he often found it incredibly difficult to be in a group setting, at the end of 2010, Jared, whom most staff had rarely heard utter a single word, began to sing. In a clear, strong voice, he sang 'Michael, Row Your Boat Ashore' to an audience of several hundred people.

Sharing understanding

For her efforts at the school, Bella was named the Equity Trustees Not for Profit CEO of the Year for Australia in 2005. The award included a $20 000 travel grant. Bella sourced an additional $15 000 from Darrell Fraser, then Deputy Secretary of the Victorian state education department's Office for Government School Education, a great supporter of the school's pioneering work. These funds allowed Bella, Pam Russell and Martin Comte to attend the 2006 United Nations Educational Scientific and Cultural Organisation World Conference on Arts and Education in Lisbon, Portugal.

With Bella, Pam and Martin each attending different sessions at the conference, the group was able to discuss and share a range of different perspectives and ideas. Bella, Pam and Martin were impressed by all the ways in which the arts were being used to assist disadvantaged impoverished children, but they agreed that one significant population had been overlooked.

'We didn't see any examples of the arts being used to help children with intellectual disabilities,' Bella says.

In an effort to share what PPSS had learned about the arts and special education, in 2008 the school hosted the International Symposium on Re-imagining Special Education through Arts Education and Arts Therapy (RiSE Symposium). The conference drew dozens of contributors and hundreds of attendees from across the globe. Everyone at the RiSE Symposium had success stories about creative programs, novel teaching strategies and inspiring ideas. But front and centre were the stars of PPSS—the teachers, paramedical specialists, therapists and students—all ambassadors of the success of a fully-serviced school with an integrated program offering arts-based education.

Bella retired from PPSS at the end of 2008 and Robert Newall was appointed principal in 2010. Both are convinced that PPSS's pioneering approach can work elsewhere. 'You don't need to be a big school to do this,' Bella says. 'We just happened to have a big dream.'

We hope after reading this book, school staff—both those in special education and those in mainstream schools who work with children with additional needs—will gain understanding, skills and strategies for helping children with intellectual disabilities. We hope principals may discover another dimension to what they already provide and consider a rich curriculum designed around the needs of children. We hope policymakers may glean valuable insights that will be of assistance as they allocate scarce resources and identify priorities in education. And finally, we hope that parents will better understand the importance and relevance of engaging their children in the arts, at school or in extracurricular activities, and recognise that the arts not only have intrinsic value, but are crucial tools to help children learn far more than we ever imagined.

PPSS is a model that works on many levels and deserves to be replicated. But first, to provide a context for what is happening at PPSS, we include papers from two leaders in education (see Chapters 1 and 2). These papers were originally delivered at the RiSE Symposium in 2008.

Following these contextual chapters, the book moves on to explore the fully-serviced school model, integrated services and the Integrated Services Committee, the Visual and Performing Arts Curriculum and how art changes the brain, and proof of the efficacy of the school's approach.

PPSS Staff 2011

Main photo: [Top] Katie Brice, Bec West-Conley, Ben Lorenz; [Back] Anne O'Brien, Jo Stavros, Chisato Shigemi, Sean Proko, Anto Marston, Dan Dinnen, Michelle Hilder, Marg Connell, Ross Denby, Susanne Mackey, Cathy Rendall, Craig Osborne; [Middle] Roger Yelland, Eric Bentelzen, Stephanie Carson, Jacqui Chalmers, Helen Doyle, Clare Duncan, Peter Njaroge, Ann Harris, Yvonne Joannides, Tash Adler; [Front] Anita Bragge, Clare Redenbach, Anna Johnson, Kate Yelland, Ellen Pettitt, Kristy Parks, Janet Hutchinson, Susie Fowler, Robert Newall, Yvonne Miller, AnneMarie Bolger, Deb Fisher, Yael Arinz, Juliet Cooper, Skye Mathews, Anna Korczynski.

Portraits (left to right): [First] Chris Edmonds, Jo C-Scott, Amy Laity, Annemarie Bennett, Jim Yarwood, Margaret Gawler, Elaine Maher, Anne Braun, Ally Randall, Georgie Labb; [Second] Sarah Haji, Dr Carl Parsons, Amanda Musicka-Williams, Pauline Vassallo, Tony Spiker, Simone Boness, Margie Lauchland, Anne Schwarz, Kathy Nicholson, Christine Vlasic; [Third] Nicki Seguna, Adina Kleiner, Kathy Tierney, Carmel Connellan, Ros Jennings, Alison Druce, Sarah Wright, Julie Weston, Elise Denton, Barbara Nicholls.

Chapter 1
Don't hang your dreams in a closet: Sing them, paint them, dance them, act them ...[1]

Martin Comte

In 2006, I attended a UNESCO-sponsored conference on the arts in Portugal with Bella Irlicht, principal of PPSS, and Pam Russell—two of the major forces behind the RiSE Symposium.

After the conference in Lisbon ended I arranged to spend a few weeks in Paris. On leaving my hotel in Lisbon for the airport I was conscious that traffic congestion was sometimes a problem, so I left very early in fear of running late for the plane. As it turned out it was a perfect run and I arrived at the airport several hours before the plane was scheduled to depart. But clearly I was not the only one afraid of missing my plane: the airport lounges, not the roads to the airport, were congested. There were people everywhere and not enough seats.

I couldn't bear the thought of waiting for three or four hours in such a congested lounge, trying to find a seat and knowing that if I left it even for a few minutes I would lose it. So when I went to check-in I gave the lady behind the Air France counter my Qantas Club card, knowing full well that Air France, with whom I was flying, was not a partner airline of Qantas and that I would not be able to use the Air France Lounge. Nonetheless, I thought it was worth a try. Anything was worth a try, given the crowded airport. But, as I knew would happen, the nice young

---

1   This is an edited version of the Opening Address of the International Symposium on Re-imagining Special Education through Arts Education and Arts Therapy, delivered at Queen's Hall, Parliament House, Melbourne, on 26 July 2008.

lady told me that there was no reciprocal arrangement between Air France and Qantas for using each other's airport lounges. I put on my most disappointed face and for some reason it touched her because she asked me if I had any other card. I looked in my wallet and, apart from my credit card, I only had a Victorian Seniors Card—a card that Australians will know is given to anyone over the age of 60 who is not in full-time employment. But I was desperate. The lady asked me what sort of a card it was and I said, quite truthfully, that it was a special card given by the Government of Victoria to senior people—people who are special. After all, it does look extremely official and imprinted on it are not only the words the 'Government of Victoria' but also the Victorian Coat of Arms. I could tell that the lady behind the desk was curious. And then I read to her and myself what the card actually says: 'The holder is a valued member of our community. Please extend every courtesy and assistance.' Signed, the Government of Victoria. Even I was impressed for the first time! Indeed an air of confidence descended on me as I emphasised again that this card was reserved for very special people: senior people. And I was one such person. A senior person so highly regarded by my government that they gave me a special card to take with me wherever I went to let people know that I was 'a valued member' of the community. And the government— my government—wanted anyone who met me to extend to me 'every courtesy and assistance'. By now the lady behind the desk was extremely impressed. She asked if she could take it to show to her supervisor to see if this might in fact enable me to access the Air France Lounge.

Shortly after she came back beaming, with her supervisor alongside her. They were going to allow me into the Air France Lounge. And they asked me for my boarding pass that had just been given to me. They wanted to change it. They upgraded me—from economy to first class. And before I knew it, somebody was picking up my hand luggage and escorting me to the lounge—not the normal Air France Lounge, but the Air France President's Lounge! It was obvious that they were extremely impressed to have such a dignitary who travelled with a special card given by my government that said that I was a valued member of the community and deserved every courtesy and assistance. Believe it or not, I was blushing.

This true story has made me think how nice it would be if the sentiments on my Victorian Seniors Card, that I got simply by reaching the age of 60, could be extended to those children who were the subject of the RiSE Symposium—children who need special education, children who attend special schools, children who, for whatever reason, do not attend mainstream schools. Does my government regard each one of them as 'a valued member of our community'? Does my government ensure that they are extended 'every courtesy and assistance'? Indeed, does the community in general regard these young people as valued members of our community to whom every courtesy and assistance should be extended? And what, further, does my government think of them when they become adults? How does it show that it values them then? Does it extend them every courtesy and assistance in adulthood?

This chapter, 'Don't hang your dreams in a closet: Sing them, paint them, dance them, act them ...' has a two-pronged focus.

Firstly, it implies the importance of educators and decision-makers allowing themselves to dream; it implies the importance of educators and decision-makers giving themselves permission to dream. Because I believe it is through dreaming and re-imagining that we can open our minds to more possibilities. It is through dreaming that we can unleash our creativity and find new or at least better solutions to the way we think and act. Dreaming is relatively easy: the hard part for some is permitting themselves to do it. It can take courage to allow yourself to dream. But once you have dreamt, putting your dream into reality can be the easy part. Sadly, too often we leave our dreams in the closet because we convince ourselves that they could never be brought to fruition. I hope that this book will encourage you to take your dreams off the coathanger and share them. In the process I hope that you will dream some more. And I hope that others will dream with you. And in sharing your dreams you will also be sharing your sense of the world—your reality.

The second focus implied in the title of this chapter is that all children should be encouraged to give expression to their dreams and, where appropriate, use the arts as a tool to achieve this. The arts, I believe, have a power, a potency, to unlock traditional barriers to expression and communication. The arts allow children to say what words do not. The arts allow—indeed, the arts facilitate—the expression of states of mind, feelings and emotions. The arts, in other words, are not just important because of their aesthetic qualities, but also because they provide us with valuable tools for developing a child's potential outside the realm of aesthetics. That is, the arts have a vital therapeutic role to play in the development of children with special needs—far more perhaps than they do with children in mainstream schools. (But, parenthetically, I often think it is a pity that the therapeutic role of the arts is not acknowledged in curricula in mainstream schools.) The arts, indeed, allow all of us to represent our reality in ways that words are often unable to do. In a sense, the arts also allow us to hide behind masks—literal and metaphoric ones—as we express our thoughts, our needs and desires, as we explore relationships, and as we deal with difficulties. The arts in education and in therapy are commonly seen as a way of 'making meaning'. And in the process we are allowed, indeed encouraged, to play. The arts also allow us to express our dreams. The arts allow us to bring our dreams to life. And not only this: the arts enable us to test our dreams in a safe and secure environment. Can you think of a more powerful tool for the development or education of children? I can't.

Where, then, does arts therapy sit? Put simply, arts therapy is a process that depends on some form of engagement with one or more art forms with a view to affecting or facilitating change—physical change, psychological change, emotional change, relational change, social change and so on.

Is the role of the arts therapist closer to that of teacher or closer to that of artist? Maybe—probably—this is a question that shouldn't even be asked. The important thing is that both of these roles (teacher and artist)— if they exist at all—are subservient to the role of therapist.

This, then, raises for me the question of what the relationship should be between the arts therapist and the arts educator—the music therapist, for example, and the music teacher; the art therapist and the art teacher. What is certain is that their roles are substantially different. It concerns me sometimes when I come across special schools where the distinction would not appear to be clearly understood.

I am also concerned that we tend to compartmentalise arts therapy sessions from the mainstream of teaching and learning. We often segregate arts therapy sessions. I know that Bella was committed to assimilating arts therapy into the mainstream of what happens in the classroom. I personally believe that the principles of arts therapy should much more strongly underscore all that occurs in the classroom.

One of the strongest images that I have carried around in my mind for 20 years is of a rather nervous four-year-old boy. He had no sight; he had been blind since birth. I watched as a dance therapist encouraged him to explore space—to walk around a room that had obstacles in it and to feel secure in each footstep he took. He was introduced to the dance therapist who picked him up and sang to him. And as the therapist sang he began dancing around the room with the boy in his arms. The therapist deliberately brushed past the two brick pillars or columns in the room so that the boy could feel them, while secure in the therapist's arms. The therapist then did the same with some chairs that had been randomly placed in the room. He did the same with the doors. For the first time the little boy began smiling. He began singing. He was dancing. He was exploring space. He was gaining confidence. And when the therapist put the small boy down and held him very close, with them both facing the same direction, together they moved around the room as if they were one person. The young boy began laughing. The therapist laughed. The boy's mother, who was watching, also laughed. Then, all three of them hugged each other and moved around the room together. The therapist had engendered such a strong sense of trust in this tiny boy. Next he faced the boy and they held hands and danced around the room, sometimes the therapist danced backwards and other times the boy danced backwards. And then the boy danced with his mother. And what was particularly brilliant was that the boy began initiating the direction of the movements. The therapist played some music on the CD player and they all danced. If I hadn't known otherwise I would have thought that a miracle had been wrought in that session and the boy had re-gained his sight. But I need to stress that this was just a normal day for the therapist and not every day unfolded with such success. And not every child responds so quickly, so openly and so freely.

It concerns me that in Australia—more so than in some other countries—we tend to think in terms of individual arts therapies (dance therapy, music therapy, art therapy, drama therapy) rather than working across the arts therapy modalities. As Phil Jones (2005) has posed in his excellent book entitled *The Arts Therapies: A Revolution in Health Care*, 'Does it make any difference to the client if they have access to only one art form or to a variety of art forms within the therapy?' (p. 96). In other words, does it matter which modality (or combination of modalities) is used in therapy?

And let us not lose sight of the fact that there are different emphases within the arts therapies. To quote Jones again, 'It is not as if there is one approach that dominates the arts therapies as a whole, nor even a single approach within one modality such as art therapy or music therapy' (p. 221). Personally, I prefer an Expressive Arts Therapy approach, where the therapist works across the individual arts modalities. But in engaging in the debate we must be careful not to lose sight of our mission—and that is to work with special needs children in order to help them fulfil their potential. As an aside, I think that my dance therapist who worked with the four-year-old blind boy was more a creative arts therapist.

But I have a much more important concern than that of singular arts therapy approaches versus multi-arts approaches in therapy. I am greatly concerned that teachers who teach in special schools are not given additional—or adequate—training in the arts so that they can effectively and with confidence use the arts as tools in the development of children. Tools for their physical development. Tools for their emotional development. Tools for their psychological development. Tools to help them communicate. Tools for making meaning. Tools to assist them to make sense of their world. In other words, the arts as therapy. And so I ask you to consider the ideal training in arts and arts therapy for teachers and others who work with special needs children.

But to take it a step further, I want to argue for a model of teacher education that enables teachers to dream and, if appropriate, to take their dreams out of the closet and translate them into reality when working with children. My model would ensure that teachers of special needs children know how to shift their dreams from coathangers to practical classroom experiences using the arts with great confidence. Such a model will require teachers to become much more familiar with the arts as tools of learning and change. And equally it will require teachers to be better trained to be creative in their thinking and teaching; it will, indeed, require them to dream.

And when I suggest that teachers should be encouraged to dream, let us not lose sight of the fact that some of the greatest inventions in the world, some of the most successful ventures, have occurred because people gave themselves permission to dream. I think that René Descartes was only half right when he said, several hundreds of years ago, 'I think, therefore I am' (1644). What a pity that he didn't say 'I think and dream, therefore I am'! But he was suspicious of dreaming. Dreaming, sadly, has long been frowned upon in western education. Pity the poor child who is accused of 'daydreaming' in class. Yet in Australia we have the example of our own Aboriginal cultures where the Dreaming or the Dreamtime is a core element.

Allow me to share another concern in relation to arts therapy in special school settings. I'm disappointed at the relative lack of ongoing school-based research into arts therapy in this country; research that focuses on the use of arts therapy with children in special schools and other related settings. I strongly believe that school systems, universities and individual schools themselves could do much more in this regard.

Forgive me for indulging myself in expressing such a long list of concerns—but events such as the RiSE Symposium give me hope that some of these concerns might be discussed and addressed.

The RiSE Symposium was organised around three key perspectives: firstly, philosophy: what is the nexus between the arts, arts therapy and special education?; secondly, program implementation: how can teachers develop skills and understandings to use the arts and arts therapy in special education?; and thirdly, leadership and strategy: how can we shift understanding at a community or policy level to advocate for the importance of the arts and arts education in special education?

Although I have already made passing reference to all three of these perspectives, I would like to tease out a little more the third perspective of leadership and strategy because it is the one, it seems to me, that holds the key to achieving the aims that are implicit in the first two perspectives. This third perspective relates to government, decision-makers and the community acknowledging—not on a plastic card, but in reality—that special needs children are valued members of our community and accordingly we will offer them every assistance. This must become enshrined not only in government legislation but equally in practice. And it must be enshrined in our collective community psyche. It is an issue not only of leadership and strategy but also of advocacy.

Unfortunately, overall, the status and provision of the arts in Australian schools have not improved over many decades. We have several state and federal government reports dating back to at least the mid-1970s that lament the provision and status of the arts in schools, from preschool through primary and secondary school. This of course is not to deny impressive pockets of success—wonderful pockets of success—but that is simply what they are: pockets of success.

For me—and I have no doubt for you—the importance of the arts for us as human beings is self-evident. But if we look at school curricula and practice, this importance is rarely given due acknowledgement. Nor is the importance of the arts sufficiently acknowledged in the training of preschool, primary (elementary) or special school teachers. One only has to look at the amount of time given to the arts in teacher education today compared to 30, 40 or 50 years ago to see how much things have changed for the worse: today, considerably less time is given to the arts in the preparation of teachers who work at the preschool and primary school and special school levels. And Australia is not unique in this respect.

Let us for a moment try to imagine what life would be like without the arts. Twenty years ago some colleagues and I developed a brochure that said: 'Imagine Life Without the Arts'. I want to share the spirit of this brochure with you.

Imagine life without the arts:

- no music
- no paintings
- no theatre
- no posters
- no photos
- no CDs
- no films
- no DVDs
- no wallpaper
- no novels
- no poems
- no short stories
- no Christmas or birthday cards (well … maybe boring ones)
- no jewellery
- no buskers
- no dance parties

And so on …

What a dull world it would be.

Of course it would be a dull world without the arts. How poorer humanity would be. I'm sure you won't find a bureaucrat or decision-maker who would openly disagree—yet, when it comes to education or special education, and when it comes to the training of preschool, primary school or special education teachers, there is much reason for thinking that we live in a world where the arts really don't matter much at all. Surely we won't have to resort to a plastic card that says 'The arts are valued members of our curriculum community. Please extend them every courtesy and assistance within the curriculum.' Signed, the government.

I have argued, of course, that not only are the arts integral to education but, further, that the arts as used in therapy are integral to special education. In advocating for arts therapy to be more pervasive in programs dealing with special needs children it is of course important that we identify exemplars of best practice. And I stress that I'm not merely referring to examples of schools where children have a weekly art therapy, dance therapy, music therapy or drama therapy session and then it's back to the main business of the day. No! I'm arguing for something much stronger where the arts as therapy are used as tools by teachers and assistants in the classroom in the normal course of teaching on a daily basis. I'm arguing for the principles and practices of the arts therapy modalities to be much more integrated or assimilated into daily classroom practice. I'm arguing for all teachers and others who work with special needs children (not just the therapists) to be trained to regularly employ at least basic arts therapy skills and practices in order to better facilitate children's growth and development.

Strong words! But this is precisely the thinking that went into the design of a new curriculum for all children at PPSS a few years ago.

The necessity for advocacy for special needs people was brought home to me in quite a different and disturbing context from a most unexpected source less than a year ago. I have a dear friend from my university days, Carol MacInnes. We've been friends for 44 years. We both love good food and wine and sometimes we go to extreme ends to indulge ourselves. For the past two years we have been specialising in the pubs of Melbourne and beyond in search of the perfect pub meal.

In 2007, Carol broke her hip and had to have an operation to insert a special pin to help it mend. The operation was successful. But what was not successful was the treatment she received from then on. Medical and paramedical staff saw not the Carol who has managed to be mobile throughout her much of her life with the use of a walking frame, but instead someone who has a history of breaking countless bones in her body since birth and who now was flat on her back in a hospital bed. It was apparent to Carol that the medical staff were only concerned to ensure that she could sit up in bed so that she could read and watch TV. It was clear that they then envisaged that she would eventually go home and spend the rest of her life in a wheelchair. And this was the start of Carol's problem. She had great trouble convincing doctors and paramedics that she was used to doing more in life than simply sitting up. She has successfully mobilised herself in a frame for years. She has taken herself overseas in her frame. She goes shopping in her walking frame. And, as I said, we go out wining and dining on a regular basis accompanied by her walking frame.

But no—it seemed as if there was a consensus on the part of the staff in the hospital that as long as Carol was able to sit up their work was complete. Carol tried telling them just how mobile she had been before her fall. But it fell on deaf ears. Now let me stress to you that Carol is extremely articulate. And she's very experienced in stating her needs. She has a Bachelor of Music degree, having majored in both piano and flute. She has taught these instruments in schools and privately for many years—but her spirits were diminishing on a daily basis because no-one was accepting the fact that she intended to be just as mobile after her recovery as she had been before her fall. Throughout her life she has had the will and fighting spirit to overcome adversity. But now Carol was failing. I visited her in the hospital one day when she was at rock bottom. I went home feeling depressed and extremely angry. And then I sat down at my computer and typed up the Carol MacInnes Manifesto. It gave her background. It listed her many successes as a student, as a teacher and as a performer. It noted what a rich family and social life she enjoys. It detailed the types of activities that she was used to participating in.

And then I returned to the hospital with multiple copies. We hatched a plot. From then on Carol ensured that every doctor, nurse, physiotherapist, occupational therapist, medical student (and there was a steady stream of them) was given a copy of her manifesto. What's more, she made them read it before she would allow them to examine her, before she would allow them to work in therapy with her and before she would answer any of their questions. The turnaround was almost immediate!

Why am I telling you Carol's story? It's obvious, I'm sure. Here is someone who leads a very active life who at a time of crisis was losing courage to advocate for herself. How much more do special needs children need to be protected and supported to ensure that appropriate advocacy takes place on their behalf rather than them being assessed simply on appearance as to their potential or capabilities?

Every special needs child—not just every senior citizen—must be guaranteed the right to be regarded as 'a valued member of our community'. Every special needs child—and not just every senior citizen—must be extended 'every courtesy and assistance'—not, metaphorically speaking, simply assisted to sit-up in bed so that they can watch TV.

You see, I want teachers, decision-makers, educational bureaucrats and governments to dream of the possibilities for special needs children. I want them and all of us to dream and re-imagine what special education in and through the arts could do for children. I firmly believe that despite the advances that have been made we can still do much more for children with special needs than we are doing today. These children have every right to be valued members of our community and to be treated throughout their lives as such. They must not be marginalised. And I don't have to tell you that there is overwhelming evidence to suggest that social inclusion can positively affect mental and physical health in a variety of different ways. It is therefore in the interests of special needs children and the broader community that as children and adults they be allowed to participate as fully as possible in mainstream society. This must be at the forefront of our deliberations as we re-imagine special education.

As we seek to re-imagine special education I want to share just one other thought with you. Increasingly I'm attracted to the notion of 'gifting'. That is, giving a present—a gift. 'Gifting' is a term that is not used a great deal in education—but I think it should be. We talk mainly of teaching. But the notion of 'gifting' has a certain appeal—especially, it seems to me with respect to special education. 'Gifting' is a relatively small and even marginal stream of thought in the fields of philosophy, ethnology and even sociology. For me, the notion of gifting is closely aligned with a concept of dignity that all special needs children must feel. 'Gifting' implies a reciprocity that I find enticing: the notion of the receiver of a gift (e.g. a student in relation to a teacher) also giving back. The 'giver' (the teacher) is also the 'receiver'; the teacher then again gives back. Gifting also entails, it seems to me, a sense of generosity that is not normally discussed in relation to teaching and learning. Gifting is not simply the one-way process that we often associate with teaching and learning. I'm personally attracted to the notion of teachers being both givers and receivers—not simply givers, which is how we often portray the teaching–learning process. The notion of gifting, I suggest, acknowledges the uniqueness of each child: teaching on the other hand, is more commonly associated with inter-changeability—the notion that one child is basically the same as another. So in re-imagining special education I would ask that you give some consideration to a broader concept than merely one of teaching and learning.

I must stop this as I'm just indulging in yet another of my dreams—another of my re-imaginings—in relation to special education: the dream that maybe we could re-conceive the concept of special education—indeed, education, teaching and learning, in general.

You see, I want all governments to ensure that special needs children are valued members of their community and extended every courtesy and assistance. And if anyone in education needs to dream it's not only those involved directly in special education, but also the governments and bureaucrats whose decisions can have such a profound effect on the extent to which we can dream, and, indeed, whether we can do it in colour, in stereo, in 3D. Whether, in fact, we really can sing our dreams, paint our dreams, dance our dreams, or act our dreams.

Chapter 2
In the national interest

Brian J. Caldwell

In recent years I have gained a deep appreciation of special education, arts education and arts therapy and their importance in the overall scheme of things as efforts are made to achieve a world-class system of education. I am in awe of what has been achieved in special schools.

The Australian Government is committed to an education revolution. It is my contention that the education revolution will not succeed and that educational transformation will not occur until all schools adopt or adapt some of the strategies that are evident in the best special schools, especially those that build approaches to learning around the arts.

Personalising learning

A powerful illustration is provided in personalising learning, which has become a mantra in efforts around the world to secure success for all students in all settings. While there are many definitions of personalising learning and many practices are encouraged, a common feature is that there should be a learning plan for every student, that the progress of each student in this plan should be monitored frequently, that support is available to get the student back on track should he or she fall behind, and that at least one teacher should know the student well and serve as a mentor. Accounts of good practice in personalising learning are emerging.

On a national scale, Finland is invariably considered an exemplar in this respect (Barber & Mourshed 2007). As is widely known, Finland performs best out of the nations that participate in the Programme for International Student Assessment (PISA). Finland stands out because the overall mean level of performance of 15-year-olds is one of the highest of all nations but also because the gap between its high- and low-performing students is relatively small, and there is only a weak association between level of socio-economic disadvantage and level of performance. In the widely-used jargon, Finland is 'high quality—high equity'.

Millions of frequent-flyer points are being accumulated as leaders in education fly to Finland to learn the secrets of its success. Among many factors, one stands out: namely, no student is allowed to fall behind. Each student is monitored so well that the moment he or she falls behind, special support is provided, either one-to-one or in small groups. This is what is meant by special education in Finland. Teachers who provide such support receive additional training and are paid more. About 30 per cent of all students in primary and secondary schools are supported in this way.

Why do we need to fly to Finland to fathom this out? I was challenged on this when I wrote an article for one of Tasmania's daily newspapers (Caldwell 2008), referring to the high level of performance of schools in Finland, highlighting in particular the special education support I have just described. An alternative opinion was published a few days later in which the author exclaimed that 'If I hear any more about the wonders of Finland and how we should be emulating it, I think I might throw up' (Walker 2008, p. 32).

Okay! If not Finland, why not special education in Australia or special education in other nations to model best practice in personalising learning? There is a personal learning plan for every student. Staff monitor progress on a daily or weekly basis. Staff work in a team to ensure that needs are diagnosed and action is taken. High levels of skill and commitment are required. Here is how Dr Carl Parsons (2007) describes the work of the Integrated Services Committee at Port Phillip Specialist School that involves the principal, two assistant principals, social worker, psychologist, director of integrated services (Carl Parsons), speech–language specialists, occupational therapist, physiotherapist, music therapist, art therapist, drama therapist and various members of the special education teaching staff and classroom assistants:

> For a discussion of each student, the team that comes together to discuss the student's needs may be different. For example, one student may require input from the physiotherapist, the occupational therapist, the art teacher, the physical education teacher and the swimming teacher.
>
> The Integrated Services Committee has the opportunity to identify areas of need for a student and his/her family. Practical approaches can

be discussed and plans of action set. Often family members are invited to attend meetings. Parents, teachers, or any therapist can ask for a 'case review' for a student at any time. Often there is linkage with external agencies and service providers so that the school is providing the central link for meeting a student's needs. Using this integrated approach, each student's individual needs can be identified, discussed with the relevant people, and appropriate and specific actions can be taken to ensure that each student reaches his or her maximum potential. (Parsons, 2007, p. 18)

It is understandable that Carl Parsons declares that 'integrated services are the heartbeat of the school'.

My point is this: why travel to Finland to learn how to do it when world-best practice in personalising learning is at hand? There is value of course in travelling to Finland even though the context is different. But there is also value in visiting the best special schools. In both cases there must be adaptation to the wider school setting. I see no difficulty scaling up to a school of 1000 or 2000 students the particular approaches that are working so well in special schools of 50 or 150 students. It will mean remarkably different approaches to the delivery of services, but that should be part of the education revolution.

Mobilising all of the resources in a community

Outstanding practice in special schools also presents the best example we have yet seen of how a school can mobilise all of the resources that are available to it to achieve transformation: success for all students in all settings. In 2007 and 2008 we undertook a study in six countries to determine how schools that had been transformed or had sustained high performance had built strength in each of four kinds of capital and aligned them through effective governance to secure success for their students. We were seeking to validate the model illustrated in Figure 2.1. The findings were reported in *Why Not the Best Schools?* (Caldwell & Harris 2008).

Intellectual capital refers to the level of knowledge and skill of those who work in or for the school. Social capital refers to the strength of formal and informal partnerships and networks involving the school and all individuals, agencies, organisations and institutions that have the potential to support and be supported by the school. Spiritual capital refers to the strength of moral purpose and the degree of coherence among values, beliefs and attitudes about life and learning. (For some schools, spiritual capital has a foundation in religion; in other schools, spiritual capital may refer to ethics and values shared by members of the school and its community.) Financial capital refers to the money available to support the school. Governance is the process through which the school builds its intellectual, social, spiritual and financial capital and aligns them to achieve its goals.

The model in Figure 2.1 was the starting point for the International Project to Frame the Transformation of Schools. There were two stages. The first called for a review of research on the four kinds of capital and how they are aligned through effective governance. An outcome was the identification of 10 indicators for each form of capital and for governance. The second called for studies in five secondary schools in each of six countries: Australia, China, England, Finland, the United States and Wales. The project was carried out by Educational Transformations with different components conducted by international partners with funding from the Australian Government and the Welsh Assembly Government.

Fifty indicators—10 for each kind of capital and for governance—were identified. I will consider two sets here in the context of special schools—intellectual capital and social capital—and illustrate briefly my contention that outstanding special schools model world-best practice.

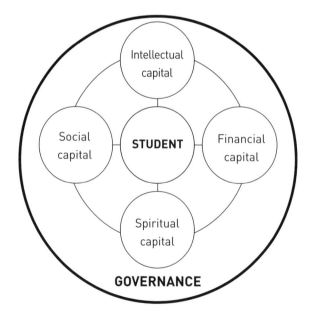

Figure 2.1   Alignment of four kinds of capital

16

Intellectual capital

The 10 indicators of intellectual capital are:

1 The staff allocated to or selected by the school are at the forefront of knowledge and skill in required disciplines and pedagogies.
2 The school identifies and implements outstanding practice observed in or reported by other schools.
3 The school has built a substantial, systematic and sustained capacity for acquiring and sharing professional knowledge.
4 Outstanding professional practice is recognised and rewarded.
5 The school supports a comprehensive and coherent plan for the professional development of all staff that reflects the school's needs and priorities.
6 When necessary, the school outsources to augment the professional talents of its staff.
7 The school participates in networks with other schools and individuals, organisations, institutions and agencies, in education and other fields, to share knowledge, solve problems or pool resources.
8 The school ensures that adequate funds are set aside in the budget to support the acquisition and dissemination of professional knowledge.
9 The school provides opportunities for staff to innovate in their professional practice.
10 The school supports a 'no-blame' culture which accepts that innovations often fail.

Outstanding special schools including and especially those that place arts education at the centre perform well on each of these indicators. A superb illustration is the PPSS approach to integrated service delivery I referred to earlier. Indeed, this approach comes closer than any I have encountered to an educational counterpart of the best of clinical approaches in health care.

Social capital

The 10 indicators of social capital are:

1 There is a high level of alignment between the expectations of parents and other key stakeholders and the mission, vision, goals, policies, plans and programs of the school.
2 There is extensive and active engagement of parents and others in the community in the educational program of the school.

3 Parents and others in the community serve on the governing body of the school or contribute in other ways to the decision-making process.

4 Parents and others in the community are advocates of the school and are prepared to take up its cause in challenging circumstances.

5 The school draws cash or in-kind support from individuals, organisations, agencies, institutions, philanthropists and social entrepreneurs in the public and private sectors, in education and other fields, including business and industry.

6 The school accepts that support from the community has a reciprocal obligation for the school to contribute to the building of community.

7 The school draws from and contributes to networks to share knowledge, address problems and pool resources.

8 Partnerships have been developed and sustained to the extent that each partner gains from the arrangement.

9 Resources, both financial and human, have been allocated by the school to building partnerships that provide mutual support.

10 The school is co-located with or located near other services in the community and these services are utilised in support of the school.

Outstanding special schools perform well on each of these indicators. In respect to the fifth point in the list above, I have found no counterpart in any school in any country to what has been accomplished at PPSS in terms of the support it has mobilised for its 'education through the arts' initiative (Port Phillip Specialist School n.d.). No fewer than 36 organisations and institutions provide support of one kind or another, including some of Australia's largest companies and leading foundations and trusts. In addition there are numerous instances of individual support from the wider community.

Arts education and personalising learning

Consistent with the approach I am taking, my purpose at this point is to place arts education and arts therapy in a broader context, especially in response to the question: 'How can we shift understanding at community and policy levels to advocate for the importance of the arts and arts therapy in special education?'

Arts education and arts therapy demand that learning and the support of learning be personalised. Therefore, we are adding world-best approaches in arts education and arts therapy to world-best practice in personalising learning. To be blunt: this is a double whammy for policymakers who wish to transform schools and design and deliver an education revolution.

At the community level, considerable attention has been paid to the work of Oliver Sacks, Professor of Clinical Neurology at Columbia University. The title *Musicophilia: Tales of Music and the Brain* (Sacks 2007) has sunk into public consciousness. It is a powerful affirmation of the arts and arts therapy in special education. He refers to some people with autism:

> ... who may be unable to perform fairly simple sequences involving perhaps four or five movements or procedures—but who can often do these tasks perfectly well if they set them to music. Music has the power to embed sequences and to do this when other forms of organisation (including verbal forms) fail. (p. 327)

Sacks pays particular attention to people with Williams syndrome (fewer than one in ten thousand children) who have a 'strange mixture of intellectual strengths and deficits', with most having an IQ of less than 60. He writes that 'even as toddlers, children with Williams syndrome are extraordinarily responsive to music', observing that 'the three dispositions which are so heightened in people with Williams syndrome—the musical, the narrative, and the social—seem to go together' (p. 329).

Sacks explains how the condition involves the 'micro-deletion' of fifteen to twenty-five genes on one chromosome (out of twenty-five thousand or so genes in the normal genome) and concludes that the syndrome affords 'an extraordinarily rich and precise view of how a particular genetic endowment can shape the anatomy of a brain and how this, in turn, will shape cognitive strengths and weaknesses, personality traits, and perhaps even creativity' (p. 331).

Arts education and the national curriculum

What is central to success in special education as far as arts education is concerned should also be central to education in general. It was therefore startling that there was no place for the arts and arts education in the first stage of writing an Australian national curriculum. In a discussion paper to frame consultations on its work, the former National Curriculum Board (now the Australian Curriculum, Assessment and Reporting Authority) declared that students' schooling 'should help develop a sense of themselves and Australian society, a capacity and disposition to contribute effectively to society, and the knowledge, understanding and skills with which to work productively and creatively' (2008, p. 2).

The National Curriculum Board's remit in the first instance was to develop a national Kindergarten to Year 12 curriculum in English, mathematics, the sciences and history, and only then to turn to geography, languages other than English and the arts. This omission has now been addressed.

The initial sidelining of the arts reflects the bifurcation in the disciplines of learning that has existed since at least the 19th century. Paul Johnson (2006) draws attention to the problem in his book *Creators*, where he describes the work of men and women of outstanding originality, including Geoffrey Chaucer, William Shakespeare, Johann Sebastian Bach, Jane Austen, Victor Hugo, Mark Twain, Pablo Picasso and Walt Disney. In an affirmation of what has been accomplished in arts education in special schools, he declares that 'creativity is inherent in us all' and 'the only problem is how to bring it out' (p. 1). In special education, it is brought out in ways that were not accomplished and could not be accomplished in a curriculum that sidelines the arts. Johnson believes that 'the art of creation comes closer than any other activity to serving as a sovereign remedy for the ills of existence' (p. 3).

Looking back over the centuries, Johnson reminds us that 'throughout history, no real distinction was made between the exercise of skill or even genius in the arts and science'. He recalls that 'Renaissance studios, especially in Florence … buzzed with artist scientists', concluding that 'the truth is that until the nineteenth century, there was a single culture of learning' (p. 277).

One of the most influential people in shaping the curriculum of schools is Harvard University's Howard Gardner. He developed the idea of 'multiple intelligences' more than 25 years ago, in which music and movement, in particular, find their place. These intelligences are named: linguistic, logical–mathematical, spatial, bodily–kinaesthetic, musical, interpersonal and intrapersonal. There would be few initiatives in curriculum development that have not drawn on his work. It is noteworthy that Gardner includes the arts among requirements for learning in schools:

I believe it is essential for individuals in the future to be able to think in the ways that characterise the major disciplines. At the pre-collegiate [school] level, my own short list includes science, mathematics, history and at least one art form. (2006, p. 31)

In the national interest

One of the major pitfalls in policy and practice in education has been the rigid compartmentalisation of much of what we do. Examples include 'special education' and 'normal education'; 'public' and 'private'; and 'the sciences' and 'the arts'. Schools have also tended to lock out many who would like for all the right reasons to give them support of one kind or another. The view that business has no place in the schools of the nation is one example.

Thankfully, things are changing and I commend the then Deputy Prime Minister Julia Gillard for advocating along these lines in the 2008 John Button Memorial Lecture. It is probably the best articulation of what constitutes the education revolution we have heard to date. She called for a 'raging debate' about 'how our education system compares to the best in the world', 'how to ensure that every school is a great school' and 'how to ensure every child gets an excellent education' (Gillard 2008).

Julia Gillard referred to the quip, often attributed to John Maynard Keynes, that 'When the facts change, I change my mind. What do you do?' (Gillard 2008). I suggest that the facts have changed about special education. It is time to re-imagine special education and draw lessons for all schools in respect to personalising learning, drawing on the resources of the whole community, transforming approaches to learning through the arts and arts therapy, and creating a place for the arts in the national curriculum. It is in the national interest to do so.

Chapter 3
A fully-serviced school

It is important to note that while the innovations at Port Phillip Specialist School are extraordinary, the student body of the school is typical for a specialist school. During her tenure as principal of PPSS, Bella Irlicht became convinced that, to give those students the best possible education, the school needed to hire not only excellent special education teachers, but also many other specialists. That was the genesis behind her transforming PPSS into a 'fully-serviced' school. Dr Carl Parsons, director of integrated services at PPSS, details the wide range of intellectual and physical disabilities of children at the school, and explains why the school adopted the fully-serviced model.

The philosophy behind a fully-serviced school

Carl Parsons

PPSS is a Victorian government school that caters for 150 children from two to eighteen years of age with a wide range of intellectual disabilities. The number of students at the school fluctuates between 135 and 150 per year. Figure 3.1 shows the distribution by age of 150 students in 2009.

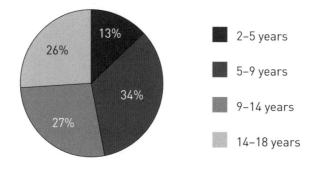

Figure 3.1   Age of PPSS students

All students at the school have an intellectual disability. This means that they have a history of delayed or disordered development and have participated in a series of tests, including an IQ test that has resulted in an IQ of 69 or below, making them eligible to attend the school. The chart below shows that 48 per cent of the student population has a specific syndrome related to intellectual disability (with the largest single syndrome being Down syndrome at 15 per cent); 37 per cent has an autism spectrum disorder; 10 per cent has a physical impairment; and 5 per cent has acute medical needs.

Historically, syndromes were identified by a series of features or characteristics that people had in common. These features included physical features, medical conditions and behavioural aspects associated with the disorder. Many of the syndromes were named after the individuals who identified these features, and some were named after the major biological processes that were affected.

Since the Human Genome Project (completed in 2003), there has been a greater emphasis on identifying the specific genes and the type of genetic deletions, duplications or changes in genes and where they occurred on the genes, and this has resulted in the current identification of syndromes. In 2009, as part of our integrated services case reviews, I made a list of the types of syndromes that were found in students in PPSS. The names and chromosomes associated with these syndromes are listed in Table 3.1.

It is important to recognise that individuals with intellectual disabilities come with a variety of other complicating problems. This is often referred to as comorbidity. Comorbidity is the presence of one or more disorders in addition to the primary disorder. Thus, people with many of the

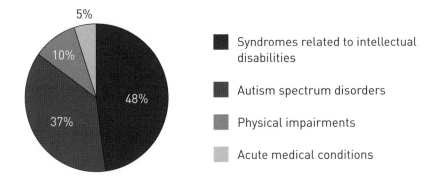

Figure 3.2   Disabilities of PPSS students

Table 3.1 Some types of syndromes at PPSS

Syndrome name	Chromosome/gene	Discoverer	Year	Comments
Angelman's syndrome	Chromosome 15	Dr Harry Angelman	1965	Chromosome 15 has been linked to autism. Most people with Angelman syndrome show characteristics of autism.
Apert syndrome	Chromosome 10	Eugene Apert	1906	
CHARGE syndrome	Chromosome 8	B.D. Hall	1979	
Cri du chat syndrome (also called Lejeune's syndrome)	Chromosome 5	Jerome Lejeune	1963	
Crouzon syndrome	Chromosome 10	Octave Crouzon	1912	
DiGeorge syndrome (also called Sphrintzen syndrome)	Chromosome 22	Angelo DiGeorge	1968	22q11.2 deletion.
Down syndrome	Chromosome 21	John Langdon Down	1866	Easily diagnosed by facial features. Once thought to be the most frequent cause of intellectual disability. It is now known that other disorders are more common despite being less commonly diagnosed: e.g. fragile X syndrome, for which children are rarely tested; and foetal alcohol syndrome, for which there is no genetic test.
Edwards syndrome (Trisomy 18 or Trisomy E)	Chromosome 18	John Edwards	1960	

Syndrome name	Chromosome/gene	Discoverer	Year	Comments
Ehlers-Danlos syndrome	Chromosomes 1, 2, 5, 6, 7, 9 and 17	Edvard Ehlers and Henri-Alexandre Danlos	1901	There are six types of this syndrome. Chromosome 9 accounts for 50 per cent of cases.
Foetal alcohol syndrome	Not genetic	Paul Lemoine; Christy Ulleland; Ken Jones and David Smith	1968–1973	This is thought to be the most frequently undiagnosed reason for intellectual disability, and that many cases of intellectual disability are caused by alcohol use by the mother early in the unborn child's development. There is no genetic test for foetal alcohol syndrome.
Foetal valproate syndrome	Chromosome 1	DiLiberti	1984	High incidence of autism spectrum disorder.
Fragile X (also called Martin–Bell syndrome & Escalante's syndrome)	Chromosome X	J. Purdon Martin and Julia Bell; Herbert Lubs; Frederick Hecht	1943	This syndrome is the most common single-gene cause of autism spectrum disorder.
Galactosaemia	Chromosomes 1, 9 and 17	F. Goppert	1917	There are three types of this syndrome. Chromosome 9 causes the most severe form.
Hunter syndrome (also called mucopolysaccharidosis Type II)	Chromosome X	Charles Hunter	1917	
Hurler syndrome (also called mucopolysaccharidosis Type I)	Chromosome 4	Gertrude Hurler	1919	

Table 3.1   Some types of syndromes at PPSS (cont.)

Syndrome name	Chromosome/gene	Discoverer	Year	Comments
Jacobsen syndrome	Chromosome 11	P. Jacobsen	1973	11q deletion.
Klinefelter syndrome (also called XXY syndrome)	Chromosome X	Harry Klinefelter	1942	
Landau-Kleffner syndrome (also called infantile acquired aphasia)	No specific gene found	William Landau and Frank Kleffner	1957	
Neurofibromatosis (also called von Recklinghausen disease)	Chromosomes 17 and 22	Fredrich Daniel von Recklinghausen	1882	
Noonan syndrome	Chromosome 12	Jacqueline Noonan	1971	
Patau syndrome (also called trisomy 13 or trisomy D)	Chromosome 13	Klaus Patau	1960	
Phelan-McDermid syndrome	Chromosome 22	Katy Phelan and Heather McDermid	1988	High relationship to autism spectrum disorders.
Pierre-Robin syndrome	Chromosomes 2, 4, 11 and 17	Pierre Robin	1923	Often co-occurs in foetal alcohol syndrome.
Prader-Willi syndrome	Chromosome 15 (seven genes)	Andrea Prader and Heinrich Willi	1956	It is believed that as many as 75 per cent of cases are undiagnosed.
Rett syndrome	Chromosome X	Andrew Rett	1966	Unique to girls; high incidence of autism spectrum disorder.

Syndrome name	Chromosome/gene	Discoverer	Year	Comments
Rubinstein-Taybi syndrome	Chromosome 22	Jack Rubinstein and Hooshang Taybi	1963	
Sanfilippo Syndrome (Mucopolysaccharidosis Type III)	Chromosomes 8, 12 and 17	Sylvester Sanfilippo	1963	Problems with Chromosome 17 account for most of these cases.
Smith-Lemli-Opitz syndrome	Chromosome 11	David Smith, Luc Lemli and John Opitz	1964	High relationship to autism spectrum disorders.
Smith-Magenis syndrome (also called 17p syndrome)	Chromosome 17	Ann Smith and R. Ellen Magenis	1986	
Tuberous sclerosis (also called Bourneville's disease)	Chromosomes 9 and 16	Désiré-Magloire Bourneville	1880	Up to 60 per cent of cases have autism spectrum disorder.
Williams syndrome	Chromosome 7	J.C.P. Williams	1961	
Wolf-Hirschhorn syndrome	Chromosome 4	Herbert Cooper and Kurt Hirschhorn	1961	

syndromes listed often have dysmorphic facial features that allow others to recognise that something is wrong or that they are different. They are prone to increased health problems (including susceptibility to infections) and medical problems (including increased heart, lung and kidney problems, and increased need for medications), and major sensory difficulties (including loss of hearing or vision, difficulties regulating body temperature and an increased or decreased need for sensory input). Many people with intellectual disabilities have epilepsy or seizure activity of some sort. They can also have associated motor impairments, problems with feeding and swallowing, difficulty sleeping, increased problems with attention, memory and learning. Some have depression, anxiety and mental health issues. The point of all this is to recognise that each individual has a complex range of needs that must be understood in order to provide appropriate remedial services.

It should also be noted that many of our students do not have a genetic diagnosis. This is due to the fact that many have not been tested genetically; for example, it is thought that 75 per cent of students with Prader-Willi syndrome are never diagnosed. This is due to the fact that genetic testing is just beginning to be a routine procedure in medicine. There are also some students who have foetal alcohol syndrome, which, while one of the most frequently occurring syndromes, is often undiagnosed and has no genetic base. There is an increasing number of students with autism entering the school each year. No single genetic array has been found to cause autism, but we know that large numbers of children who have autism also have a genetic disorder as well; for example, many individuals with fragile X syndrome also have autism spectrum disorders. This is also true for tuberous sclerosis, as up to 60 per cent of these individuals have autism spectrum disorders (Curatolo et al. 2004).

Characteristics of intellectual disabilities

About three per cent of the general population has an intellectual disability and a majority of intellectual disabilities are caused by genetic factors. Environment can also be a contributing factor. Intellectual disabilities are caused by structures, chemicals and processes in the brain not working normally. Thus, the brain does not respond normally to many learning conditions. Indeed, students with an intellectual disability:

- have difficulty focusing attention on relevant cues
- have difficulty paying attention for long periods of time (although they may attend for lengthy periods for a few highly selected activities)
- have problems memorising (especially materials they are not interested in or don't understand)
- may lack motivation
- learn more slowly than their non-affected peers
- have slowed processing skills affecting their ability to respond rapidly
- have a reduced overall capacity to learn (thus we need to ensure that we teach the most relevant skills)
- often require even basic tasks be taught, whereas their non-disabled peers may learn a skill 'automatically'
- have problems understanding consequences and thus may lack understanding about care, safety and common-sense choices
- have difficulty understanding 'the future'
- have major problems generalising skills from one environment or situation to the next.

Each student with an intellectual disability will show a particular profile or pattern of learning that needs to be discovered and used to the student's benefit. Table 3.2 gives some ideas about the effects of intellectual disabilities on students. This chart is used to teach all of our staff about the approximate abilities of our students. This helps staff to get a better appreciation of the skills that our students can learn. Without this information, teachers often try to teach subject matter that may be too difficult or unrealistic to achieve.

In order to assist the learning of students with intellectual disabilities we need to find ways to increase their focus and sustain their attention; find what motivates them, and their unique interests and talents; and allow additional time to learn tasks with numerous repetitions. Learning tasks must be broken down into very small bits. Time to complete activities is increased; time to respond is increased. We find that it helps a student to practise activities in numerous situations, and that engaging a student's entire body in activities promotes better learning. Staff must consider the relevance of tasks. We teach routines and situation-specific information, then train in new situations; use visual and aided-language

Table 3.2 Approximate abilities of students with intellectual disabilities

Level	Intelligence quotient (IQ) range	Ability at school age (5 to 18 years)	Ability at adult age (18 years and older)
Mild	52–69	Can learn up to about eight-year-old level by late teens; can learn some appropriate social skills. Often struggle with literacy and deep learning. Mostly do activities by rote and routine.	Some can learn social and self-help skills, but may need guidance and assistance throughout life. Can learn skills specific to a situation and with support or supervision. Lack the ability to generalise from one situation to another.
Moderate	36–51	Can learn simple routines that are taught repetitively. May develop to about a five-year-old level. Often not able to learn academic skills.	Need continual supervision and guidance throughout life. Unable to live independently.
Severe	20–35	Often developmentally no more than three years old. Benefits from habit training. Goals should be self-help oriented, e.g. toilet training, dressing, feeding.	May contribute partially to self-care under complete supervision. Learning extremely slow.
Profound	19 or below	Extremely low skills. Often functioning below a two-year-old level.	Very limited self-care; usually needs extensive care.

displays to help understanding; teach about the 'here and now', not the future; teach about concrete rather than abstract topics and concepts; and use extensive reinforcement and feedback. Staff members are patient and persistent, but also consistent. We set high standards but all goals must be realistic, attainable, measurable and lead to some important skill that will improve the student's quality of life, ability to learn or ability to be independent. When we teach a new skill it takes time and extended practice in numerous situations before it becomes part of the students' repertoire of skills and abilities. We practise these skills in classrooms, specialist programs and in activities during the school day.

Developing a fully-serviced school model

In the mid 1980s through to the 1990s, there were frequent calls for school reform. During this time, most of the advocates for reform suggested learning outcomes could be improved by adjusting the curriculum. Unfortunately, curriculum reform alone does not address many of the barriers to learning that students and families have.

In general (although not at PPSS), students who have difficulty learning are often referred to support services outside of the students' school. This can include numerous therapy programs, counselling or tutoring done away from school. The student in need of some specialised help may get a range of different services, but these are not usually coordinated by professionals, and service providers often act independently of each other. There is often little or no linkage with the school. Teachers, aides and volunteers who might work with the student are given little advice or training on how to deal with the student. All of this contributes to maintaining an enterprise that is narrowly focused, fragmented and oriented to discrete problems. To address these issues, the concept of fully-serviced schools was conceived by Howard Adelman (1993), Joy Dryfoos (1994) and Carol Calfee, Frank Wittwer and Mimi Meredith (1998). This concept had been tried in a few places in the United States and the United Kingdom. While there was not much research-based evidence that it was a better model than the existing system of external support services, people who used the fully-serviced model felt it had an enormous impact on service delivery and service coordination: intuitively it seemed better.

PPSS was the first school in Australia to develop a fully-serviced school model. The fully-serviced school concept as developed at PPSS by Bella Irlicht required that a multidisciplinary group of services be available at the school. Bella's basic theory was that a child who had a sore tooth, or who hadn't eaten a good breakfast, or whose parents were suffering from stress, wasn't going to get all she or he could out of school unless those problems were addressed. Bella objected to a system that she believed 'siloed' services: health under this roof; psychology under another; education under a third, and so on. Bella went on to create a far more comprehensive school than the one she inherited. She understood that for a student with specialist needs, it was likely that the family also would have additional needs. She wanted to ensure that the student could have the majority of her or his needs met at the school. This often required bringing in specialists from a range of disciplines to help families and teachers more fully understand the intricate details of the student's disability. Bella understood that a full range of professionals could help to maximise learning for each student. She identified the range of professionals she needed, she found funding to employ them and she set up mechanisms to make sure these professionals worked collaboratively.

Today, PPSS delivers extensive services which are provided within a framework of a special education school program. There are approximately 65 staff members, with a range of expertise. On-site there are 20 classroom teachers who are qualified in special education as well as 20 assistants who support teachers in the classrooms. There are also six specialist curriculum teachers who provide programming for art, dance, drama, music, physical education and swimming. The therapy team services include art therapy, counselling, dance therapy, drama therapy, hydrotherapy, music therapy, occupational therapy and an independent living centre for practising daily living skills, physiotherapy and a full gymnasium, psychiatry, psychology, psychotherapy, social work, sensory processing programs, a swimming pool and specialist swimming instruction, speech–language therapy and audiometry, a technology centre for computers and computer-assisted-learning devices, and a toileting program. In addition to these internal services, there are extensive linkages to local hospitals, doctors and dentists, podiatrists, schools, independent organisations and family support groups. These linkages ensure that staff, students and families can access relevant services and the school has up-to-date information on services and availability. This range of services (full services, if you will) is coordinated by the Integrated Services Committee (which is the focus of Chapter 4 in this book).

~~~~~~~~~

Among the many factors that make PPSS a fully-serviced school is that it serves the community by providing education to very young students. While many specialist schools begin at age five, PPSS accepts children as young as two years old into its Early Education Program (EEP). These children attend two three-hour sessions per week. There are three classes within the EEP—two taught by Simone Boness and one taught by Yvonne Miller. The teachers and teaching assistants of each class collaborate in the classroom with PPSS's speech–language pathologist, occupational therapist and physiotherapist for at least an hour each week. Following is an illustration of how the fully-serviced school philosophy can be put into practice with the youngest children attending PPSS.

In practice: Start small, think big

On entering PPSS, the first impression through the multi-paned windows is a blur: cheery colours, dappled sunshine, high ceilings. The walls throughout the school are decorated with self-portraits, collages, abstracts and other student artwork, as well as myriad photos of children. The school is neat but not fussy: a snug, happy, welcoming place.

The children attending the PPSS Early Education Program enter the school through a separate door, around the corner from the school's main entrance.

'It's very confronting for families to have a child go to a specialist school,' explains teacher Yvonne Miller. 'It takes time to adjust. We offer a sort of sheltered harbour. Some of our students will go on to mainstream education, and others will continue at a specialist school. Regardless, these children deserve a special place of their own, where their accomplishments are celebrated.'

Children like David. At two-and-a-half years old, he wasn't making his 'milestones'—developmentally, he lagged far behind his peers—and he began having seizures. What was wrong? David was hospitalised for so long that his mum Emily sewed him a hospital gown for each night of the week. Decorated with sequins, ribbons and feathers, she nicknamed the most elaborate one his 'Friday-night happy-hour' gown.

Emily's humour and resilience were sorely tested when doctors finally gave the family a diagnosis. They said David had Angelman syndrome— he was missing his 15th chromosome. Doctors told the distraught parents their first-born child would never walk, never talk, and would experience global developmental delay. Emily, who was nursing a newborn baby, was considered to be at such risk from learning the diagnosis that she says she was put on suicide watch.

'They didn't think I was dealing with the situation, which wasn't true,' Emily explains. 'I just wanted to leave hospital and take him home, to live with us and his little brother. I didn't want to be told all the things he couldn't do. I wanted to see all the things he could do. We enrolled David at the school because he loves music, and we liked the school's emphasis on the arts. Also, his teacher Yvonne doesn't say "no, David can't do this or that". She tries to figure out a way.'

The Early Education Program at PPSS has helped to foster David's development, but according to Yvonne, among the most remarkable features about the program is that it exists at all.

'When I began teaching, it was during the 1970s, and people with disabilities were in institutions,' Yvonne says matter-of-factly. 'Families didn't have a lot of options. They either sent their children away, or had to teach them at home. There wasn't proper schooling for them. And certainly not at this age—no-one offered teaching for young children with a disability, even though that's such a great time to start!'

Neurologists and educators know that assisting children early is the best way to help them acquire skills and reach their fullest potential. In his landmark book, *The Brain That Changes Itself* (2007), author Norman Doidge provides solid evidence that the brain is far more able to adapt and change than previously thought—welcome news for parents of children with brain disorders. There is ample evidence that the brain is especially 'plastic'—able to re-route around a damaged area, or have one region of the brain take over another region which isn't functioning properly—in the earliest months and years. When it comes to dealing with brain injury or intellectual disability, the earlier that specialised teaching and training can be employed, the better.

During her time at PPSS, Yvonne has taught in the junior school, and now in the EEP. In her work with two- to five-year-old children, Yvonne knows that the best way to assist the brain to re-route is to build on each student's strengths rather than to try to 'fix' a deficit. Like other teachers at the school, she believes in transparency: parents need to know what teachers are doing, so that what is learned at school can be reinforced and amplified at home, and vice versa. Yvonne says the play environment reveals how children adapt and change as they use both new and familiar equipment. Consequently, her program is constantly evolving as she monitors the children's play and extends their development of new skills.

Because many of the students at PPSS are non-verbal, the school keeps a communication book for each child, in which teachers record for parents their child's individual weekly focus (e.g. take part in dancing the 'Hokey Pokey'), as well as some of the activities their child does each day (e.g. jumped one centimetre off the floor with both feet for the first time in dancing, used the rope bridge, used the toilet, said new words). As many of the children are unable to tell their parents about their day, the communication book is one way to share information.

Yvonne and her assistant read and update the book daily. As they see the parents each morning, the communication in the book tends to be one-way, from the EEP to parents. Parents sometimes discuss with Yvonne activities from home that she can share in the classroom (if provided with photo or reminder to show the child as a prompt). When parents flag issues with Yvonne, these are initially dealt with over a cup of tea, with the parents and Yvonne bandying ideas back and forth to try new things to help resolve the issue. However, if the issues are large, Yvonne may either brainstorm with a psychologist, social worker, occupational therapist, speech–language pathologist or physiotherapist at the school to find the best solution or, with the parents' knowledge, bring the issue to an Integrated Services Committee meeting.

This dialogue is both casual and crucial: it creates a bridge between PPSS and parents, so that it's possible to troubleshoot small problems before they escalate. Izzy is throwing massive tantrums when her sister comes home from school? Mum should try to ignore this attention-seeking behaviour, and instead give extra attention to her sister. Sam has discovered how to use wetting as a weapon? It's not the first time. Here's a copy of a helpful DVD you won't find at the local video store: *Tom's Toileting Adventure*.

Then there's Ginny, who has autism and has only begun talking. At first it was adorable when she mastered that line from her book on frogs: 'Jump in the pond on a rainy day.' But now she repeats the same phrase endlessly—delayed stereotyped echolalia. Yvonne discusses the development (and it is a development, even if it is annoying) with Ginny's parents, offering ideas and proven strategies (such as adding more words to an already existing phrase that Ginny is using) for her parents and EEP staff to extend the language that exists.

'When a child has an intellectual disability, Mum and Dad need our support, just as much as their child needs assistance,' Yvonne says. 'They face overwhelming demands on their time. If there are other children, that's another issue, because a child with additional needs will often get more attention than their siblings. And of course, there is tremendous grief. We call it, "the loss of the imagined child". We're here to support the entire family.'

Yvonne makes sure that each parent is in contact with Ros Jennings, the resident PPSS social worker.

'Much of my work happens in just that way,' Ros explains. 'A behaviour will crop up in a classroom, and we check to see if it is also happening at home. The therapy team and I can offer strategies in both places. Ultimately, we all need to be on the same page.'

The goal at PPSS is to help children and their families not just to cope, but to thrive.

A keen photographer, Yvonne has decorated the walls with photos of her students at work and play. Yvonne is quick to recognise and record the achievements, large and small. After a lot of work put into getting her physically ready to do so, Dana walked across the floor for the first time! Working on his fine motor skills, Jeremy cut up his food at morning tea and was rewarded at the end with eating the fruit! Sandy loves the sensory input she gets from painting, and her newest effort is gorgeous!

To assist her students, Yvonne's kinder classroom contains specialised, state-of-the-art equipment: a trike complete with a body brace, given by one of the families; several swings and hammocks on ropes and pulleys; and other equipment brought in as needed.

Adjacent to the classroom through a sliding door is a darkened sensory room with soft pillows on the floor and a lava lamp. Skye Purtill, the school's occupational therapist, has collaborated with Yvonne on creating a space with targeted sensory information that helps students to maintain a calm, alert state when they need a break from the stimulation of the classroom. Many children with an intellectual disability are either 'sensory avoiding'— they dislike too much noise or activity, or the way certain things feel, taste or smell—or are 'sensory seeking', in which case they crave various sensory stimuli. Providing students with sensory input as a preparation can assist them to increase their attention to other tasks. Classroom assistant Moira Davis makes sure these children get a chance to play with the Moon Sand, or perhaps wash dishes to indulge their love of water play. Both options can relax students and help with sensory processing, so they can attend to lessons.

But one of the most powerful tools in Yvonne's toolbox is neither complicated nor expensive. It is accessible, adaptable and often low-cost or free.

That remarkable tool is music.

It is impossible to overstate the role of music at PPSS. It is ubiquitous. As the children arrive at Yvonne's class, the gentle chants of Native American music may greet them, creating a calm start to the morning. Or on livelier occasions, they may be serenaded by the dance rhythms of Cuba. Each week for a 35-minute session, the school music teacher comes to the room to entice the children into playing music, singing, listening and using musical instruments. She also sees some of the children individually or in small groups in her role as music therapist.

As a classroom teacher, Yvonne has made an art of discovering which songs aren't just great musically, but also are easy to adapt for drama, dance and the visual arts.

'Take "Row, Row, Row Your Boat". I can do so many things with that song!' Yvonne explains. 'In fact, I have built an entire curriculum around it. The children who can sing love the catchy tune. But the arts are essentially non-verbal. That's what works so well in a specialist school setting! The children who can't speak can shake a tambourine or a bell, or bang a drum. The song also has great action—you can use your whole body, and that's great for our children.'

Yvonne uses Pippa Goodhart's 1997 version of the classic 'Row, Row, Row Your Boat' as an example. In the song, children propel their little craft to an island, where they find myriad animals, and engage in all sorts of vigorous activities.

'We use the power and rhythm of the song, and the fun of singing, to get children to *do* things,' explains Yvonne, 'The children not only row, they kick, splash and leap. And we're not just doing, we're also *pretending*. Pretending is important developmentally.[2] Well, in the song, we're pretending to be sailors. Or monkeys. Or snakes.'

---

2   Garvey (1977), Giffin (1984), Howes (1985) and Howes et al. (1989) have all demonstrated that pretend play is important for learning.

Props and costumes help. A sand pit becomes the beach; a lion costume helps a child get into character, as well as work on dressing skills.

'School should be fun,' Yvonne smiles. 'Occupational therapy sounds like work. But creating an island of your own is a game. We have the children draw a boat, make masks with papier-mâché, create animals with lots of feathers and construction paper—it's much better than trying to "isolate a pincer grip" in some textbook way. As for a child who can't draw, we might use their foot or handprint in paint to make the leaves on the tree. Everyone is involved. There's lots of fine motor work in this— skills that will help them with everything from writing their name to tying their shoes—but the children never notice. They are absorbed in creating something special.'

Music unlocks an invisible mental gallery where children can hang words, numbers and concepts.

Yvonne sums up this way. 'We sing. We dance. We draw the sets. We act out the song,' Yvonne ticks the list off on her finger. 'There you have it—the arts! But these aren't just separate classes—this is just how we teach.'

~~~~~~~

Another example of the fully-serviced nature of PPSS is its pioneering 20-year partnership with a nearby mainstream kindergarten. The result of that collaboration is that 10 children who are enrolled in the PPSS Early Education Program actually attend the Port Melbourne Uniting Church Kindergarten.

~~~~~~~

In practice: Inclusion kindergarten

On a day of wild weather, the wind and rain mean there will be no chance to use the climbing frame or play in the sandpit. The Port Melbourne Uniting Church Kindergarten children and staff are unconcerned. They sit cross-legged in a circle on the class's large rug, gazing attentively at kindergarten director Heather Larter, who holds aloft a large maroon ball of wool.

Heather says to the children, 'I'll roll the ball across the circle to someone who is opposite me. That person will then roll the ball to someone different that is opposite them.'

There's a noisy chorus of 'Pick me!' accompanied by pleading looks. Heather sends the ball rolling to Genna, who listens to the instructions to pinch the thread between two fingers of one hand, as she uses the other hand to roll the ball across to another child, Paige. Now Paige grabs a piece of wool and sends the ball careering to Tom, who in turn spins the wool to Naveen.

'Is the ball getting bigger or smaller?' asks special education teacher assistant Anne-Marie Bolger.

'SMALLER!' cry several children at once.

'Look, look!' interrupts one little girl.

'That's right, Genna,' nods Early Education Program teacher Simone Boness. 'Do you see the pattern?'

These children have been captivated by a spectacular web. A web so large that when their collective spinning project is complete, each child has a chance to scramble underneath, to a chorus of delighted squeals and giggles. 'You look like spiderlings. That's what baby spiders are called,' says Heather.

But suddenly, above the happy squealing, there is an ear-splitting shriek. A small girl sitting next to Genna suddenly stands up, hands held tightly by her sides, eyes closed, screaming. Simone doesn't miss a beat. She walks directly to the child, drops to her knees in order to position herself at eye level and looks directly into the face of the child.

'Inside voice, Grace,' she says firmly. The young girl lashes out, as if to hit the teacher. 'No hitting, Grace. Hands down,' Simone continues in a strong, calm voice.

The other children turn to look and Heather explains that Simone is helping Grace to express her needs in a quieter manner. Heather diverts them. 'Now, who will be a spider next?'

As the other teachers make sure the game resumes, Simone gently escorts Grace away from the circle. It isn't easy. Grace throws herself to the floor and begins kicking the ground.

Simone stands nearby, just out of range, not looking at Grace, until the emotional outburst subsides a bit. Then she moves in, helps the little girl to her feet and says, 'Grace, let's go to the playroom for you to settle yourself.'

Simone leads Grace to the second playroom within the larger kindergarten classroom. As Grace sits on a chair, Simone sets what's called a 'Time Timer'. This device not only gives a numeric indication of how much time has elapsed, but a visual cue as well. The number of minutes shows up as a red pie-shape, a wedge which gradually gets smaller as time elapses, until the timer dings. This will indicate it's time for Grace to return to her activity.

Grace keeps a close eye on the timer and Simone stays with her, avoiding any engagement. In the quiet room, Grace's breathing has settled and she appears noticeably calmer.

'All finished,' Simone says clearly, making no more mention of the behaviour. 'Now let's go back to the circle.'

While the other children have moved onto other activities, Simone takes Grace back to the abandoned spider game, where she directs her to help roll up a bit of wool.

'That's better!' she says encouragingly, now giving Grace a smile. 'Where would you like to play now?' And then Grace has been reintegrated into the class.

Grace has been diagnosed with a developmental delay connected to complex epilepsy.

'Sometimes the excitement of the other children overstimulates Grace,' explains Simone. 'When that happens, we need to withdraw Grace, both for herself and so she doesn't hurt or upset the other children. When her quiet time is over, we make sure Grace rejoins the activity she left, so she completes the activity without distress.

'We also make sure her time apart from the rest of the class is brief, because our goal is to have children with additional needs be part of the mainstream classroom. After all, this is an inclusion kindergarten.'

Indeed, while this classroom looks much the same as any high-quality kindergarten classroom, there is that major difference—a difference woven into the design and make-up of this kindergarten's programs.

The Port Melbourne Uniting Church Kindergarten has 23 children in the three-year-old program and 25 children in the four-year-old program. This includes five children like Grace in each program who have additional needs, ranging from Down syndrome to autism to periventricular leukomalacia (a form of brain damage in premature infants where the white matter of the brain is affected, often causing motor problems, visual impairments and epilepsy). All of those children are actually enrolled at PPSS, which is located just a block from the kindergarten. The social worker from PPSS, Ros Jennings, and the parents of each child consider if the child is best placed in the Early Education Program at Port Melbourne Uniting Church Kindergarten or at PPSS.

As for the staff, kindergarten director Heather and teacher assistant Margery Tape are employed by the Port Melbourne Uniting Church Kindergarten; special education teacher Simone and her assistant Anne-Marie are employed by PPSS.

'What makes this really special is that these are two entirely different organisations which have teamed up to create this inclusive kindergarten,' explains Heather. 'This program is valued by the staff and kindergarten committee, and by PPSS. The Port Melbourne Uniting Church Kindergarten has committed itself to providing 10 places to PPSS families because all children and families benefit from an inclusive society.'

As Heather talks about the program, the children settle down to eat morning tea. Grace chooses to sit by Genna, whom she adores. At work, play or morning tea, the children from PPSS are a part of the kindergarten and its program, and all four teachers work with all 25 of the students.

On occasion, the PPSS students are 'pulled out' for specific programs such as their weekly dance class at PPSS. Just like their peers at PPSS, these students have access to all of the school's resources, including the pool, therapists, the arts centre and gym. Sometimes the therapists come to the kindergarten to work with the PPSS students on specific goals related to activities such as speech, physical therapy or eating.

The PPSS teachers also have the opportunity to 'withdraw' an individual child, like Grace, or to take all PPSS children into the playroom. The teachers say 'withdrawing' is a useful way to help children with disabilities when they need extra help with an activity, or to consolidate a skill they've learned in the larger group.

'When we were doing the Christmas crafts, we brought the children into this room so that they could better focus on our verbal instructions,' Simone explains.

But that time apart is designed to be brief.

'If we're on our own too much, we might as well not be in a mainstream kindergarten,' Simone says succinctly.

The playroom was recently updated with glass concertina doors in a further attempt to allow viewing from one room to another.

'Teaching a wide range of children means we need to be adaptable,' Heather says. 'We talk a lot and we all get along really well. We learn from each other. Some of the PPSS children may not be able to concentrate for as long, so we might do an activity a little differently,' Heather says.

'Our children need to bounce back and forth between active and passive,' Simone chimes in. All of these teachers are sold on the benefits of inclusion kindergarten, and the team-teaching approach.

'Most days the glass concertina doors are open, allowing all 25 children to play together. We like how everyone's language and social skills improve by them being all together,' Simone continues.

'We believe it's important for our children with special needs to be able to observe and imitate other children. But we also believe all the children benefit. They gain from having children with additional needs be part of their community. It makes it easier to understand and accept individual differences. In fact, we've found that the parents of neurotypical children support this program just as much as the parents of children with additional needs! We regularly talk to the children about how we all learn at different rates.'

Some of these children will return to PPSS next year, while others will move on to a number of local mainstream schools. But Simone sees benefits for all. 'Regardless of where they go, we can offer that school information on this child, how they learn and how best that school can support them and their families,' she says.

Outside the kindergarten door, a damp and bedraggled group of parents huddles under a colourful patch of umbrellas. Heather opens the door, as the children line up to say goodbye. Genna holds Grace's hand and they walk out together.

'Mama, spider web!' announces Grace, wriggling her fingers like a spider, her emotional upset forgotten. Outside, the mums smile at each other. Clearly webs aren't the only things woven here.

~~~~~~~

Bella was determined to turn PPSS into a fully-serviced school. She had studied the first such schools in the US, so she knew the value of having a wide range of specialists available under one roof.

Since PPSS was the first fully-serviced school in Australia, the term was as ambiguous as it was appealing. When a federal education minister appropriated the term 'fully-serviced' and used it in an entirely different context, Bella capitalised on this to apply for more funding for PPSS.

Chided for her request by the minister, who pointed out the PPSS application didn't meet the government's narrow accounting definition of a fully-serviced school, Bella boldly responded that the minister wouldn't be in this situation if he hadn't borrowed the school's own terminology!

'Touché,' the minister laughed—and signed the cheque.

Bella was equally bold in choosing the therapists she wanted at the school. Take, for example, the art therapy student from La Trobe University who did a placement at the school. Bella instantly spotted the student's passion, creativity, intuition and commitment. She hired the young woman on the spot. Anita Bragge has been the art therapist at PPSS ever since. She uses a variety of media—and occasionally, even a trip to the monkey bars—to assist children with behavioural problems and developmental or psychological issues.

In their own words: The risk of drawing trains

Anita Bragge

Marley liked to draw trains. He drew trains whenever he had a chance. He drew them exactly the same way and said almost the same thing as he worked.

'Look,' Marley might say, drawing a rectangle.

'Are you watching?', as he divided the rectangle into compartments.

'Guess what it is?' Marley would look into my face and lower his voice to almost a whisper. 'It's a train.'

Marley would then return to the drawing and add the wheels, then bend over and rock over the image, his face close to the drawing.

The first time I met Marley, he engaged me in this demonstration. At this stage I was a placement student assisting the art teacher in between seeing individual students for art therapy under supervision. Marley was a tall seven-year-old with intense green eyes, wearing a helmet and looking somewhat dazed. He was demanding, talked incessantly and on seeing me asked bluntly: 'What is your name?'

'Anita,' I said.

While I helped the class into art smocks and seated them at the table, Marley continued the conversation, staring into my face. As I put children's arms into smock sleeves, he said, 'Look at me. I'm talking.' He told me the names of the members of his family and asked me to repeat them back to him. I obliged while continuing to assist the class and between exchanging amused glances with the staff.

Marley then argued against directions: to sit down, put on a smock or to listen. At each gentle reprimand, he reacted in a hurt, almost comically whiny voice with baby-like expression, a voice in contrast to his precise pronunciation and abrupt manner.

'I'm sorry, I'm sorry. Are you angry? I'm sorry. I am being good now.'

Eventually, the class was seated around the table to make puppets. As the class got under way, Marley took a pen from the table and pulled a sheet of paper from beneath the fabrics, cardboard cones, pipe cleaners and pompoms being explored by the children while the staff rotated to help students individually.

Marley was miserable and uninterested in the activity. I sat with him and he began his train drawing. I felt I had made some connection and helped settled him as he began what I later recognised as a familiar routine.

Marley reached the point in his routine where he whispered 'It's a train' and an assistant took the drawing away. The assistant explained to Marley that he was to make a princess to help tell the story with the other students. Marley argued in his hurt manner and I was stunned and confused.

He pleaded, 'Please. I just want a piece of paper. I want to draw a train.' I tried to interest him in the class activity. The art teacher and assistant said little and continued to attend to the class.

I wanted to take Marley for individual art therapy and by coincidence my supervisor recommended him to me, noting that he was a highly anxious, only child with autism and severe epilepsy who loved to draw. His classroom teacher, Yvonne Miller, told me he was obsessed with trains and required intensive one-on-one attention to engage him in any activity. She warned me about the effects of Marley's drawing dark lines, on which he 'self-stimulates' by staring closely at the lines and is then likely to have a seizure. Yvonne told me what to expect with seizures, how to respond and when to call for help. She described behaviours that indicated that a seizure was coming on and gave me strategies of what to do in the situation.

I wanted to work to expand Marley's interest in trains, initially by expanding the subject itself—trains in tunnels, going over bridges, at the station and so on. I was concerned about the seizures but felt it was

Marley's overexcitement about this image that was causing the response and that somehow we needed to alter the situation so it didn't occur. I also felt that allowing him a space to express his obsession might fulfil his need and help him to connect with other things in class. Art therapy is beneficial for conditions such as epilepsy because any expression remains present and concrete in physical space, keeping the client connected to ideas and expressions, despite memory lapses and interrupted thinking.

Children with autism often resist and pull away from any sensed expectation or interaction with others. Just sitting the child at a table can involve conflict. Art materials have a lot of learning potential through colour mixing, mark making and visual language, but the child needs to be willing and take an interest. Pushing a child to paint or handle art media is pointless. It will often make the experience negative and unpleasant. When working with children with autism, pushing is also likely to contribute to further withdrawal from adult-directed experiences.

I work to gently coax students beyond fears or reluctance, to engage in different experiences and connect with the world around them. Art materials in the art therapy context can be seen as objects in the immediate environment. Getting students with autism sufficiently calm enough to explore these materials, which involves tolerating me in their space, is a significant achievement. Art therapy connects with learning because it is fundamental for a child to take interest in things in order to interact and learn. Children with autism, however, are often in fear. They are often hypersensitive to movement, sound or visuals, particularly when these are unpredictable. Their habitual responses (such as repetitive movements or vocalisations) are often ways to block out external stimuli and withdraw rather than engage.

When working with students who have autism, I try to achieve positive experiences of interaction with others against their autistic tendencies to withdraw. I want children to experience adult interaction as something that can expand and increase their interest and enjoyment of things, rather than as someone invading personal space, making them do something they don't want to do or expecting performance or a certain response. This encourages engagement in learning, as creative teaching linked with play inspires students' curiosity in experiences within the surroundings.

For many students, art therapy is a space where they can enjoy more freedom than in class and it is often a space where I allow obsessions to be expressed. Many children at PPSS become obsessed with certain topics and want to talk about them all day. In art therapy, I often work with these obsessions to expand the imagery beyond repetitive forms and into new media, such as making models from balsa wood, modelling out of clay and sharing my drawings of the same subject to show the child different interpretations. I work to shift conversations from monologues to dialogue. Accepting other ideas is a stage in creating dialogue and acknowledging others. Beyond this stage, I work further to express my own interests, try to get a response and encourage the child's self-expression on other topics. Initially, it is a case of establishing a specific space and context to express these interests and 'get them out', in a way.

In our first session, Marley began drawing the train and in numerous sessions following he again drew the image. Sometimes he would stare at the lines and self-talk. At times he said, 'I think I am going to have a seizure.' This worried me initially, but I responded quickly with, 'No, you are not. Look up.' Then I would point out things in the distance for Marley to look at. I consciously shifted directions from the negative, from 'Don't stare,' to diversions such as 'Marley, look up at me for a minute,' or simply, 'Look up.' I would follow this with 'I want to show you something,' to take the emphasis away from the relationship to seizures.

Marley would always say early on in drawing, 'Guess what it is?' and I would respond with 'A house?'

'No.'

'Shops?'

One time I continued with as many things as I could think of and Marley began to laugh. He knew after many weeks that I knew it was a train and he was amused at the game I was playing. It was the first time I'd heard him laugh.

I focused on keeping Marley relaxed and breaking the pattern of drawing. We began to go on walks around the school in between drawing the image and I would point out things to look at: cars, trees, ordinary objects. I would encourage Marley to talk about other things. His favourite topic besides trains was to tell me the names of his family members, asking me to repeat the names back to him. After a while, to shift this pattern, I asked after family members and he began to tell me of more recent events: his grandparents going on a plane trip and his experience of going to the airport in the car.

I also worked to expand Marley's image of the train from its fixated form to introduce change, so the drawing was different every time. This was also done to break the association of having a seizure in relation to this image. In various sessions I asked Marley to draw a platform, a station, himself and passengers on the train. Over time, Marley drew trains filled with passengers and on one occasion he chose to fill the train with animals.

As months passed, Marley's drawings shifted. He drew houses, the fruit section of the supermarket, stars and flowers. Black outlines, precisely coloured-in, remained characteristic and the colours were vibrant and strong. He would go back to colour-in tiny spots he had missed and would get distressed if he went outside the lines. He liked images with repeated patterns and objects that were joined together.

One day after an individual session, I returned to the class with Marley. He was carrying a particularly beautiful drawing he had made. In class Marley showed the drawing to Yvonne and she also praised him and was delighted in the new imagery. Yvonne asked Marley to put the drawing on her desk, so it could be put in a folder and placed in his bag at the end of the day, and to sit on the floor with the rest of the class who were in the middle of an activity.

'I want to put it in my bag, actually,' Marley said.

'Put the drawing on my desk and sit with the group to read the book,' Yvonne repeated.

'No, I want to put it in my bag, actually,' Marley said.

'Put the drawing on my desk and sit down with the group,' Yvonne repeated in a clear voice.

'It's my drawing. It's mine. I want to put it in my bag,' Marley argued.

'Put it on my desk and sit down with the group to read the book,' Yvonne said.

Marley was whining. He looked to me for support but eventually complied and sat with his head down.

The incident bothered me but later I spoke with Yvonne. I've since learned that once you lay down something or say no to a child you have to carry it through, stick to it and quickly move on. Otherwise, you teach the child to manipulate situations that cannot always go the child's way. The conversation gave me a bigger picture of Marley's behaviour. Marley is controlling and anxious. He insists on getting his way about all sorts of tiny things.

I have been seeing art therapy with Marley as a means for him to regain control against his experience of constant seizures and of the anxiety connected with this. In my space, Marley has the freedom to draw what he chooses, to control the space of the page and to make marks and images that remain physically visible. While art therapy needed to continue to be a space for Marley to gain a sense of control, I needed to work with Yvonne on the social and realistic levels of not letting Marley get his way all the time, and also not setting up everything for him. There needed to be some boundaries to what Marley could control so he learned that things like mistakes and seizures are part of life and can be worked through and that not everything can be under control.

In our sessions, I had created a space where Marley had too much focus and control—an ideal situation where he was able to do what he wanted and a relationship focused solely on him and his needs. This gave him some security and we had made progress because of this, but in the broader sphere of relationships, school and family life, it may have become something he demanded all the time from others. It became time to challenge this and shift it in line with realities in life. Learning some acceptance would also help in reducing Marley's anxiety, which also often led to seizures.

Many students with autism are rigid about routines. I deliberately work to shift routines because things happen in life that mean you have to adjust and change track. This is a later stage in therapy or something I introduce with higher functioning children. Sometimes I take over for a moment and say, 'No. I don't want to make a horse today. I'm going to make a rooster' (or something I know the child likes). I work quickly hoping the child will take interest in what I'm doing, which may distract them from being upset about the change. Sometimes I make a point of ending sessions before the usual sequence is complete by taking longer with some things so we run out of time. It becomes part of therapy to get children through such events because it is a common part of life. The more unexpected experiences they have in a controlled and supported environment, the more they will be able to adapt and cope with unexpected change in other areas of their lives.

From this point on, I deliberately limited the materials in the art therapy space for Marley. Marley asked for another sheet of paper because the first line of several first attempts was wrong. I only had three sheets of paper and he had to work with the mistakes he had made. He complained. I persisted and suggested ways to work over and transform his mistakes. Over time, he learned to draw over faded texta marks with a new texta and turn a crooked line into a straight one by making it thicker.

Marley's drawings began to loosen up from rigid black outlined forms, coloured in deep colours within the lines into looser, curving forms and new shapes. More startling than the images themselves were his occasional comments, such as, 'This line is not quite right but it is okay.'

I also worked at introducing Marley to painting. Marley took to paints when he discovered colour mixing. Marley's description of events or his immediate response to things around him is often expressed with details of his visual perceptions of light and colour. Marley began painting to try out the colours in the somewhat random but symmetrical painted outlined shapes he had made for this purpose. He worked more rapidly, not noticing fragments of white in forms left unfilled. Symmetry became less important and was sometimes abandoned as he painted boats, water and things from recent memory concentrating on colour and putting in details such as 'the sparkles in the water' that he had seen when he was on a ferry.

He still articulated these changes, through comments such as, 'This line is not quite right.' These comments, the acceptance of things and ability to work with things coincided with changes in Marley. He became less anxious, perhaps more accommodating, slightly more adaptable and definitely more spontaneous. Marley is still persistent, stubborn and argumentative, but he is certainly not so uptight, rigid and serious.

An incident a few years later made me consciously shift therapy techniques to ease back from giving Marley full attention. I realised the importance of Marley learning to occupy himself, gaining independence and self-containment in his activities, and understanding other's needs.

I was at PPSS when I received a stressed call from my mum about the imminent premature birth of my niece or nephew. My mum could not talk for long; ordered me not to call anyone; and said she would call back when she could.

I waited all day and saw Marley during the last session. I was distracted and explained to him that if there is an announcement, 'Anita, telephone line one', then we have to run to the phone. Marley does not like interruptions or ending the session early. I asked if he was willing to do this. He said, 'Yes.'

I explained the situation and repeated that my mum would call. Marley asked if the baby was a boy or a girl and what its name was. I said, 'That's what we have to find out.' He smiled.

Marley painted in the room, talked through his decisions as usual and asked me to watch as he worked. I remained distracted, took a sheet of paper and told Marley, 'I'm making a painting for the baby. It is its birthday today.'

Suddenly, I realised we were working together in silence. This was extraordinary as Marley talks constantly. It was even more unbelievable when Marley looked over at my painting and said, 'I like your painting for the baby,' and pointed out the 'bright colours' he particularly liked.[3]

Disclosing this personal information in this case made me realise that I had established a routine with Marley in therapy that played into his demands for attention and an audience. The shift in my activity and sharing of personal information revealed Marley's capability to take a real interest in other people and to understand and respond to others' needs.

I met Marley's mother after school and Marley immediately told her 'Anita is getting a baby. She doesn't know if it is a boy or a girl and what its name is, but it is its birthday today and the baby is going to ring the school. Anita made a painting for its birthday.'

My mother in her excitement of the safe arrival of her granddaughter forgot to call me.

Now, while Marley paints or works on computer, I frame works to hang in the school or cut lino for students who will be making relief prints. I explain to Marley that I can't look now or I will cut myself, but I give him attention between doing my own tasks. Marley still asks constantly for me to look and watch what he is doing, but he might start by saying, 'Anita, don't cut your finger, but look. I am drawing some stairs so the animals can climb the tree.'

---

3   This disclosure of personal information reflects the intersubjective framework of the particular approach I take in art therapy. Carl Rogers (1967) included 'self disclosure' as part of the basic counselling approach from which intersubjectivity arose (Ivey et al. 1987). The openness of the therapist can be used strategically for therapeutic means.

Central to any fully-serviced school is its team of on-site specialists and therapists. The specialists and therapists at PPSS bring a range of personal and professional experiences to their roles. Take, for example, the story of PPSS music educator Tony Spiker.

As a session percussionist, Tony spent nine years in London recording with artists including Soul II Soul, Bomb the Bass, The Chimes, Eartha Kitt and Shara Nelson. For four years, Tony was the percussionist with Boy George, which involved recording, touring the world and making video and television appearances.

Later, while living in Brazil, the then-35-year-old Tony suffered a stroke, leaving him completely paralysed on his right side for some time.

Tony came to PPSS as a parent, as his daughter who has autism was enrolled as a student. When Tony approached Bella about helping out at the school, she instantly said yes. She believed employing a music educator would provide an important opportunity for the students. Tony believes his personal experiences in overcoming physical disability and dealing with his daughter's autism give him understanding and insight in his role as a music educator at PPSS.

In their own words: I've got rhythm

Tony Spiker

In 1988, I recorded on the debut album of British R&B group Soul II Soul, which sold triple platinum the following year. In 1991, I played on stage with Boy George in front of 300 000 people lining the street of the Place De la Nacion in Paris. I have had Earth Kitt belly dancing on stage to my conga playing. And in 1993, I became disabled without warning, by a random malfunction of the brain.

I had a stroke—or a left-sided cerebrovascular accident—while in Brazil. I woke up one morning completely paralysed on my right side and my prognosis was unsure. I was 35 years old.

A stroke like that makes you appreciate the difficulties a person with a disability confronts day-in, day-out, just to try and live an ordinary life. I am lucky. So lucky. Youth was on my side in my rehabilitation and the determination to play percussion again was a powerful force that helped me to get where I am today—able to play with a five per cent deficit.

I want the students I teach at PPSS to experience the same sense of pleasure and accomplishment that all of us who are musicians and performers experience when we are on stage giving enjoyment to an audience. It doesn't matter whether the crowd is in the tens, or the tens of thousands. I want the audience to forget that these kids have disabilities. I don't want people to clap because our students have special needs. I want people to clap because they are good.

My entry into the world of special needs education began on a personal level when my daughter Monique was diagnosed with severe autism at four years of age. As any parent of a child with a disability knows, such a diagnosis leaves you overwhelmed with grief and worry for your child's future in life.

When Monique entered special education she seemed happy and we became at ease with the reality that this was where she belonged. As music therapy is one of the specialist areas that has had some success, particularly with children with autism, I began to wonder whether I could contribute by working with rhythm.

I approached the principal about a putting in a couple of hours a week and working with some individual students and forming a small drum group. Bella agreed and we started a rhythm project that was an offshoot of the specialist music tuition under the supervision of the music teacher and the therapist. It soon became obvious that it was a project that had merit and could be continued on for the future. I now work with students of all ages at PPSS (excluding kinder). Our drum group and performing group meet once a week for 40 minutes, individual drum kit lessons are once a week for 30 minutes and DJ'ing is for an hour once a week.

Drums

Drumming uses both sides of the brain, aural awareness and analysis, coordination of limbs, discipline and interaction with others around you.

I decided that the ideal tool for this purpose of teaching the students to play the drums would be an electronic drum kit, and that the Roland TD-6 kit would be able to take any punishment our students could deliver.

Lessons were initially focused on identifying rhythmic ability and deciding which students could benefit from the experience. I realised that we had many students who were enthusiastic about playing drums and that for some of them it was an energy release.

The idea is to get the student quickly to play along with a music track. When they can feel that what they are doing combines with the music there is a self-esteem reward that kicks in and makes it easier for them to be taught something new or more difficult.

The drumming program utilises a range of percussion instruments, including the surdo, caixa, bongo, repique and tabla, and I try to keep the authenticity and instrumentation of the rhythm to a maximum. A Latin ensemble, for example, will include only those instruments which truly belong in that musical style and we do not improvise by adding sounds that do not relate to the authentic rhythm. By doing this we are training the student's ears to identify styles of music and learn to play the instruments with the correct hand techniques.

The drum group

The concept of a rhythmic orchestra exists in many cultures where community entertainment starts with a drum section: for example, drum ensembles of Senegal, Africa, or the 'bateria' percussion section of the samba schools of Rio de Janeiro in Brazil. The effects of many players creating one rhythm together is uplifting for the participants.

What is it that gives the player a feeling of harmony and uplifts them? It is that their simple contribution is locked into a collective rhythm that has its own force and creates its own momentum. That force physically and emotionally affects each player in a positive way, and for a student with a disability, the effect is quite remarkable.

In our drum group we use a wide range of percussion instruments that are adaptable to a crossover in musical styles: for example, our large samba drums are also used as bass drums for hip-hop beats. Students have to remember which sticks they will use and on which drum for each musical piece in the repertoire.

The key to a successful drum group is to make the student feel responsible for the quality of their contribution, rewarding them with praise when they are playing well and always focusing their energy on the next performance. Nobody wants to play badly in front of an audience.

Performing

I have always taken the approach, when working with students with disabilities, that we shouldn't want an audience to applaud or to be impressed simply because they are watching students with disabilities who are performing in front of the public. I believe my drumming group is capable enough to blow the audience away with their skill and their ability to deliver a great performance on cue. We perform three or four times a year and in doing so the students enjoy the high of a great performance, and that high gets channelled into a self-belief that is immeasurable in its positive effect on each student.

In a group situation each student has one pattern to perform, and they must listen to all the other patterns as well, but not be distracted by them so they cannot play their own pattern. If one player becomes distracted, the collective rhythm, which only exists as the *sum* of many parts, falls to pieces. The first challenge is to keep the student on task, then let them experience the feeling of how something can be achieved that is greater that what can be played on their own.

Recording

At the PPSS music department we have embarked on an ambitious recording program. This program uses the technology available in the production of modern pop music to make a recording of our students performing songs of their choice. The idea is to teach the students multi-track production of music from the ground up. This breaks the song down into its music layers, such as drum programming for the beat, bass, guitar, keyboard parts, strings and effects, and then vocals on top.

Our drum kit players will go through the process of sampling drum sounds and programming the beat. We use Musical Instrument Digital Interface (MIDI), a device that uses a digital language that allows music to be encoded and decoded in different parts, recorded, stored and played back. MIDI parts can be put together for melody instruments and our singers and choir are recorded on top. This process uses professional recording software and instruments. The process gives each student the benefit of understanding their contribution in the context of the entire project. Even if the student only played a one-bar loop on guitar or percussion, which in isolation seems to be not much, students can see how, when the whole song is put together, every contribution becomes important.

The students are always interested in the process of doing their recordings and love hearing the end result.

Trigger pads and loops

During the course of the drum program at PPSS I became interested in finding a way to include students with profound physical disability that restricts their limb movement. This came about because I could see in some students the physical strain and exertion it took to move the arms up and to reach forward.

I had experienced this personally whilst I was paralysed totally on one side following my stroke. I had to try to make my little finger move while my arm was flopped on a table. The feeling was one of complete frustration, and afterwards exhaustion. I felt that children who suffer limb palsy should not be excluded from enjoying a musical activity and I could look for a way to get them involved.

I decided to set up two electronic drum kits in a semicircle around one of my daughter's classmates Jenny, who is wheelchair-bound. Jenny has a rare and severe form of galactosaemia that affects her muscle tone throughout her body, limiting her ability to move, walk and speak. The kits joined together give her a total of 24 trigger pads to hit with drumsticks. She could hit each pad with some accuracy and a delay of two seconds between each hit.

I linked up the two drum kits together via a MIDI interface unit, which lets the signal triggered by hitting the pad travel to a laptop computer. I installed professional DJ software on the laptop to use as the host software for playing all of the loops.

The software allows the student to play layers of successive loops of music parts, one on top of the other, as they are triggered by a MIDI signal from a pad. Each loop combination is mapped to a note that a pad represents. So, for example, you might have a drum beat, a bass line and a guitar riff, each triggered by hitting separate pads.

The software is unique in that it will bring each loop combination in time with the music already being played regardless of when the pad is hit. This meant in Jenny's case she could hit a pad out of time but the signal would be held until it fit in with the music. I then programmed

24 different loop combinations of one style of music to create a musical soundscape for her to play with.

Unlimited sets of musical styles and grooves can be saved on the computer in folders for each student to access. The limit of possibilities and combinations depends only on the size of the library of loops and samples and the time available to program them.

The immediate benefit is that a student who would otherwise not be able to contribute to a musical session or group is actually playing the foundation by triggering beats and grooves that they choose themselves. Any number of students can then play along on top of the rhythm and join in the fun.

The success of these projects today and their benefit to the students comes down to a belief in the students' potential and being able to use their energy to achieve what might not have been thought possible for a student with a disability. I regard the opportunity to develop a drum program at PPSS to be a privilege and a chance to contribute to these children's lives and to show others what they are capable of doing.

Chapter 4
Integrated services

∙∙∙

It's hard to find anyone who doesn't believe in the concept of teamwork. In business, at school, in sport, getting everyone 'on the same page' is a mantra. But as any coach will tell you, turning a group into a team isn't easy.

By 1997, Bella Irlicht had assembled an outstanding staff of teachers, therapists and specialists on-site at Port Phillip Specialist School. She had completed her international research into fully-serviced education, made possible by the Churchill Fellowship she had been awarded in 1995, and so she knew that the model was built on a sound theoretical framework. The structure was in place, but Bella believed the school needed someone to implement the model—to ensure the school was making the most of every opportunity for integrating the services provided by the staff. So she hired Dr Carl Parsons, then an Associate Professor of Childhood Language Disorders at La Trobe University.

Carl had been the Associate Dean for Research and the Duty Dean of the Faculty of Health Sciences—so he had academic and administrative experience. Carl had developed a number of multidisciplinary, collaborative teams of university students from numerous universities. He had developed programs for assessment and screening in all states and territories across Australia. He was familiar with Bella's ideas and believed working at PPSS would give him, as an academic, the opportunity to get out of the ivory tower and put into practice a model he frequently lectured about.

After extensive reviews of the literature, observations of classrooms, therapists and specialist sessions, and discussions with parents, staff and external professionals, the school began to implement an integrated model of service delivery in 1999. It took four years to implement the model, and the school has in place an ongoing process of reflection, review, revision and updates to the model. Every year professional development on integrated service delivery is offered to staff.

~~~~~~~~~~

The reasons for integrated services

Carl Parsons

The notion of an integrated model of service delivery has been around for some time. Most of the early work on an 'integrated model' was done in the area of early intervention; for example, a preschooler who was known to have a disability would be sent to a range of different professionals, who all provided advice to the child's family (McWilliam 1995). The idea of a range of professionals working with families with a child with a disability was a good one (Giangreco 1986); however, as people began to do their work there was often confusion about which therapist would provide which services, and sometimes there was conflicting advice that led to confusion among families. Administrators, therapists and families became aware of these difficulties (Giangreco et al. 1991), and a few innovative service providers attempted to implement a model of what was called 'integrated services' (Anning et al. 2006; Burt et al. 1992; McWilliam & Sekerak 1995). For example, the National Individualizing Preschool Inclusion Project, funded by the United States Department of Education's Office of Special Education Programs (McWilliam & Scott 2003), had a goal to ensure that therapy services were offered to students in mainstream classrooms. Initially, the program aimed to have various therapists attend a school program and demonstrate therapy. When therapy was done in the classroom, therapists began to see each other and spoke with each other four times more often than when they provided their therapy outside the classroom. This was all seen as a positive step to help children with disabilities.

Over time, reports in the literature demonstrated that there was an increased focus on providing services through a team of multidisciplinary professionals (Phillips et al. 1995; York et al. 1990). No one professional could know everything about child development; no one person could provide all the advice or services a child with a disability needed. Having access to a range of disciplines would be more useful for families. The use of a multidisciplinary team became a part of the PPSS model.

Historically, the notion of integrated services did not consider where the program was offered. Originally, 'integrated' programs usually involved therapists coming into the mainstream school and withdrawing the student for specialist therapy programs (Ehren 2000; King et al. 2000). Professionals began to recognise the need for discussions with each other and working more closely with school-based teaching staff (Kaczmarek et al. 2000; Kemmis & Dunn 1996; McWilliam 1995; Whitmire 2002). Thus, the PPSS model incorporated the notion that the majority of therapy work needed to be embedded into the classroom.

We were aware, however, that the professional roles of therapists were often different than the roles of teachers. Teachers often worked with groups of students while most therapists were trained to work in a 1:1 model of service delivery. Teachers wanted to be inclusive, whereas therapists often felt the need to withdraw students for therapy (Whitmire 2002). PPSS decided that it needed to use a collaborative approach. Based on the research evidence about collaboration (Spencer 2005; Weiner & Murawski 2005), PPSS took the view that collaboration required teachers, therapists and specialist staff to communicate with each other on equal terms. There could be no hierarchy or divide over who was right or wrong—all professional staff were equal. Decisions about goals and priorities for treatment had to involve discussions among the relevant stakeholders. Actions and strategies had to be negotiated. The entire group was responsible for improvements in a student's learning—not just the teacher or the therapist.

Finally, Bruder and Bologna (1993) had pointed out that integrated service models in practice often lacked effective service coordination. To prevent such a failing, the PPSS model established the Integrated Services Committee, which plays a vital role in coordinating services.

Thus, the PPSS model of integrated services is unique in that it includes the following components:

- services integrated across all classrooms
- coordination of services through the Integrated Services Committee
- a multidisciplinary team which resides in the school
- a collaborative approach which requires joint decision-making by all members of each student's personalised team.

We are not aware of any other schools for children with special needs that have attempted to implement this particular type of integrated service delivery. In our view, PPSS's unique model of integrated services is an exemplar of best practice for children with special needs and their families. This section outlines the rationale for using an integrated services delivery model, provides details about integrated services, and identifies both the advantages of this model and how we have dealt with ongoing challenges. Integrating services is an appropriate strategy to use for all students, not just those with additional needs. However, research into this best-practice model needs to be continued.

Defining integrated services

The integrated service model is 'the effective utilisation of a range of professionals with different specialities (but equal status) who bring together their unique expertise to ensure that the students under their care can reach their maximum potential' (Parsons 2010). It is an interactive process that involves a range of individuals with specialist and diverse expertise generating creative solutions to problems. The creative solutions are different from those that the individual team members would have produced independently. The major outcome is to provide comprehensive and effective programs within the most appropriate context.

Integrating services means bringing them together into a whole and removing barriers, so that every part is interconnected and that every part relies on another part to work effectively to achieve a solution to a complex problem. A system that lacks coordination, is missing important components or is falling apart could be described as an example of 'dis-integrated' services.

The integrated services model in practice at PPSS

Amount of time and staff for therapy services

At PPSS, a typical school day runs from 9 am to 3 pm. Students are at school for six hours per day; however, there are a number of times during the day when students aren't in the classroom, such as at recess and lunch and during scheduled school-wide activities. For the therapists, there are about five hours a day for program time. For a full-time therapist this means that there are about 25 hours a week × 10 weeks × 4 terms, or 1000 hours of possible therapy program time during the year. Within the traditional one-to-one (or face-to-face) model of therapy, for 150 students in the school this averages out to about 6.6 hours per student for the entire year. Every student at the school has an intellectual disability. Every student at the school would benefit from some form of therapy service. Every student at school is entitled to the service.

More therapists in a particular area means more services for students or that increased quality of services can be provided. In 1999, when I first consulted at the school about the need for services, I estimated that the school, using its then-traditional model of withdrawal, would need twelve full-time speech–language therapists, eighteen full-time occupational therapists, and two full-time physiotherapists to meet the needs of 150 students with moderate intellectual disabilities. If the school were to do this, it would also probably cease to be a school because the majority of time would be spent providing intensive one-on-one therapy services— forget the curriculum, think habilitation. This is unrealistic for any school, clinical service or family.

The integrated service delivery model helps to alleviate the problem with numbers of staff and time. Thus, we increase the number of staff doing therapy and embed the therapy into daily classroom activities so that more therapy time is accumulated throughout the day. Much like an early intervention model where parents are taught to do therapy activities during daily activities at home with their child, the integrated service delivery model involves therapists collaborating with teachers and teacher assistants to set the daily classroom programs; therapists trialling the therapeutic techniques and demonstrating them to the teachers; then therapists providing continued feedback and support to adjust the programs run during the curriculum activities. This model means that students can receive therapy throughout the day, every day, during all school and curriculum activities.

All students can be involved in therapy. All therapy can be embedded into routine curriculum activities. Thus, the frequency and intensity of therapy is significantly increased.

Educationally relevant intervention with the integrated services model

All students are entitled to an appropriate education. Individuals with specialist needs require additional input from a range of specialists to help them achieve their educational goals. Students with intellectual disabilities need to focus on only a few priority goals because it is likely that if too many goals are attempted they will not achieve sufficient levels of progress. These goals are often initially different from those of non-disabled peers. At PPSS, we have identified five main areas that need to be covered in our curriculum for the types of students at the school. These areas include work on the following:

1 Motivation to learn and intrapersonal skills. This is activity directed towards learning, participating and completing classroom tasks or activities. Students who exhibit motivation to learn show interest,

engagement and persistence with academic tasks or social interactions. Students express satisfaction when learning is successful and engage in additional or renewed effort when it is successful. Students who do not have these skills or attributes must be taught them and goals may be established in these areas.

2 Pro-social behaviour and self-regulation. Pro-social behaviours are directed towards other people, effective communication skills, cooperative acts and self-control in difficult situations. Students who act in a pro-social manner take turns, give encouragement to others, compromise and share, invite others to participate in activities, volunteer to help others and listen when others are speaking. Self-regulatory behaviours are about understanding yourself and what activities create anxiety or frighten you. The student can be taught to recognise what situations, tasks or activities are difficult for them. They can be taught strategies to help them decrease anxiety and to calm themselves. Relevant goals are set for students in this area.

3 Communication and literacy. For communication, this activity involves showing recognition, listening, requesting (objects, activities or assistance), responding to questions and using routine interactive communicative exchanges. For literacy, each individual's existing reading and writing skills and abilities are used and extended with instruction from awareness to recognition of symbols, comprehension of text read by others and, for some, the ability to read words or simple texts. The primary aim is to ensure every student has functional literacy skills. Relevant goals are set by a team including parents.

4 Numeracy. Early numeracy skills involve making use of existing skills in number recognition, basic operations, simple geometric shapes and simple measurements. All of the numeracy goals are oriented towards functional numeracy—that is, so that they can be used in daily life activities, such as knowing how many plates to set at a table for four people.

5 Living skills. These goals are aimed at developing the highest level of independence possible for each student in the areas of toileting, dressing, feeding, self-care, hygiene and safety.

Each student's individualised educational goals are set by a team, which includes parents, teachers, specialist teachers and therapists. Goals aim to improve students' functioning in relevant life contexts, and therapy is embedded into the curriculum. Any intervention in the classroom is done through the curriculum, teaching, learning processes and classroom concepts, as well as through non-academic and extracurricular activities that are part of the student's fully-serviced school experience.

Advantages of integrated service delivery

There are numerous advantages to using an integrated service delivery model. I have outlined some of them below.

- Techniques can be demonstrated by teachers *and* therapists, increasing successful implementation and generalisation to other students in other learning environments. When therapy and specialist services are integrated into classroom routines, experiential activities and the teacher's instructional methods, then 'carry-over' or 'generalisation' is built into the programming effort. Thus, students, teachers and specialists do *not* have to address the challenge of transfer of skills or strategies that have been taught and practised in a separate environment, often with different materials, which might otherwise create confusion for some students and a dual curriculum for others.

- Therapy has an immediate application, as students learn and apply therapy concepts simultaneously in the same setting. When specialist programming is carefully conceptualised and planned, students begin to use treatment strategies, learned through therapy, across the curriculum, which encourages them to be more proactive and empowered learners. Opportunities for practice are available on a daily basis within the clear focus of curriculum activities.

- Collaborating teachers, specialists and therapists can build problem-solving into lessons by integrating curriculum content (what is to be learned) with intervention strategies (how to learn it). This approach helps to develop basic skills in students—like washing their hands, holding a pencil, or learning that requesting objects, activities or assistance using the Picture Exchange Communication System (PECS) can help them get what they want.

- Integrated services can benefit all students in the PPSS classroom, even those who may not appear to have a particular need for the specialised service. Some students may at some point have a need that has not been identified or isn't being serviced, or the need being addressed is at a lower priority level for them than it is for some other students.

For the student who doesn't need the service, it may appear as if he or she is simply wasting time or is being involved in an activity that he or she can already do; however, the activity could be used to build confidence, it could be altered slightly to provide an additional skill level for the student, or the student could be used as a role model for this particular skill. Working to move the student to a higher level will positively impact on the student's ability to learn.

- When two professionals are engaged in a collaborative teaching effort, one can facilitate a particular student's response or mediate learning as needed, while the other can concentrate on content. Teachers learn therapy techniques that can be personalised for their own use and have broad applicability, while specialist and therapy staff learn about the curriculum, specific teaching methods, scope and sequence of skills and expectations for the students in the class.

- Therapists and teachers can raise concerns about particular students and potential strategies for assisting each student can be arranged and trialled.

- Teachers and therapists can develop confidence in meeting the needs of individual students by establishing authentic and realistic objectives, trying alternative interventions and evaluating progress in the classroom.

- Having more than one specialist (teacher and therapist) in a classroom at any particular time promotes objective observation of students. Teaching and therapy staff benefit from these assessments of individual students' strengths and weaknesses.

Ongoing challenges

Despite the goals of integrating services, the nature of working together is that there are times when difficulties arise. Staff members have worked hard to make the integrated approach a success; nevertheless, one of the key functions of the Integrated Services Committee is to troubleshoot potential problems, and restore harmony and balance. A range of challenges is outlined below.

The challenge of interpersonal interaction

Staff at PPSS have worked hard to develop an extensive and intensive interpersonal working relationship. Staff have learned to trust and respect each other. They have learned to address conflict and differences of opinions in a positive way. However, this is a constant challenge. When new staff members come to the school, we have to ensure they learn to understand our unique model of service delivery and we have to help them learn to trust and respect others. We continually have to make sure that differences of opinions and conflict are identified and treated appropriately.

The challenge of collaboration

Collaboration is a core concept in working with students with additional needs. Collaboration among team members ensures multiple viewpoints and multiple resources and strategies are used to define and solve problems. PPSS staff understand that the unifying philosophy of integrated service delivery gives educators the means to:

- add valuable information, knowledge and skills to their existing repertoire
- increase their understanding of their students' learning
- enhance their appreciation of their students' unique interests and talents
- use interventions that respect both the students' strengths and their weaknesses.

The teaching staff at PPSS know about disabilities and treatment techniques and processes involved in teaching students with additional needs. They often don't learn this at university, but through experience and work practices. At PPSS, ongoing professional development keeps staff up-to-date on practice and recent trends in the area of special education.

Collaboration requires team members (teachers, teacher assistants, specialist teachers and therapists) to overcome their beliefs that particular behaviours, problems or treatment techniques are theirs alone, that teachers are over-burdened and that therapists should just take care of therapy. Some therapists have expressed concern that collaborative intervention makes them feel like teachers rather than therapists; they fear that their therapy has become diluted or that they have become just another pair of hands in the classroom. Ehren (2000) also documented these difficulties and suggested that therapists maintain a therapeutic focus while sharing responsibility for student success. This should be viewed as only a part of the integrated service process and one that is temporary. Through collaboration with teachers, eventually, as each teacher becomes more skilled and reassured, the therapist can gradually reduce the amount of 'hands-on' time with that particular teacher. Some therapists also share their concern that the teacher will never be able to do the job as well as the therapist. This tells us that more work needs to be done in developing the skills of the teacher in delivering therapy techniques, and in building teachers' and therapists' confidence in each other.

The challenge of shared ownership

A major problem with traditional teaching models is ownership. Traditionally, teachers have been taught that they are solely responsible for the education of students in their classroom. A collaborative model requires teachers to recognise that they cannot meet all their students' needs on their own. Thus, responsibility for improvement becomes the domain of the team and of the relevant members of the team.

At PPSS, teachers work continually with therapists and would never refuse a therapist entry to a classroom. They understand that therapists are coming into the classroom to share, learn about the students and work to assist the teacher. Teachers who have difficulty with this process are given extra support, training and time. Ultimately, however, it is essential that teachers and therapists at PPSS understand and fit into this model.

Therapists have historically worked outside the classroom. They have seen their role as providing therapy in order to make a change in behaviour. Some therapists have worked in early intervention teams where therapists teach parents to use techniques and strategies. This allows additional practice for the child and also helps parents learn strategies and techniques they can use during daily routines to maximise the benefits of the techniques. Collaboration at PPSS requires therapy staff to set programs in conjunction with teachers (as well as teacher assistants and other specialist staff like the art teacher, drama teacher, music teacher, physical education teacher and swimming teacher) and to teach staff how to use the techniques and strategies in the classroom and during routine activities during the day. Thus, therapy programs, while set by the therapists, are conducted throughout the day by teachers, teacher assistants and other teaching staff.

Coufal (1993) and Schwartz et al. (1996) have shown that classroom teachers involved with a collaborative model adapted their instructional work, which resulted in improvement in performance of students with additional needs.

Occasionally, therapists are reluctant for teaching staff to use therapy techniques. This often stems from a belief that only therapists should provide certain aspects of therapy, which can come from a failure to trust teaching staff to do therapy 'properly'. Sometimes teachers attempt to use techniques not suitable for particular students and this can concern therapists. However, these problems are ownership problems and they can be dealt with by additional collaboration and clarification. Therapists are always needed to give advice about individual student programs and ensure that the appropriate treatments are used correctly.

It is important that teachers and therapists realise that improvement and changes in behaviours and skills are the responsibility of every member of the team. This sharing of responsibility also requires an understanding that each member of the team has contributed to each student's improvement and an acknowledgement of appropriate credit to various team members. Failure to acknowledge this collaboration and input leads to problems with staff not feeling recognised or rewarded for their contribution.

At PPSS, teachers regularly incorporate the key principles of various therapies into their daily practice. Therapists work with students, work collaboratively with each other to decide on appropriate treatments and work with teaching staff to help embed the therapy into the curriculum. Students have better outcomes because of the continuity of services and the fact that they receive therapy services throughout the day. Teachers and therapists continually collaborate to develop and improve their programs.

The challenge of access to each other to collaborate

There are ongoing and persistent time constraints on staff. However, staff work hard to find the time for informal discussions, as well as scheduled meetings, through the various mechanisms (such as the Integrated Services Committee) that the school has put into place. Staff have worked on using common language so that therapists understand teacher jargon about curriculum and so that teachers understand therapist jargon (see the glossary for examples of both kinds). Goals and meetings with parents are set so that a team of relevant members is always involved in discussions for each student.

The challenge of change

The integrated services model requires teachers and therapists to function in different ways from those they learned at university or at other places of employment. To integrate services, each staff member has had to learn to involve another person (or a group of people) in assessment, planning and programming. For the staff, this change has been challenging; it is certainly 'easier' to proceed in the traditional manner of doing things on your own—teachers teaching and therapist providing therapy. The staff members have had to evolve a way of working within the school that has suited their individual needs. This is the nature of implementing a new model like integrated services.

Integrated service delivery has been a challenge because all staff members have needed to:

- engage in changes in instruction, curriculum and delivery
- connect with a range of people who have different backgrounds and different perspectives
- change their views about how to best teach a student with specialist needs
- face changes around time, energy, dissonance, discomfort and initially unpredictable outcomes
- relinquish or share control and decision-making
- accept some ambiguity in practice and outcome.

All staff members know they have an important role to play in the development of the children and the school. For most of the staff, integrating their services has resulted in a fuller recognition of their central importance and an appreciation for the power of integrated services to improve student outcomes.

~~~~~~~~

The nature of special education, and all education, is that subjects which may appear to be completely separate often overlap. From the historical and political lessons told through Leo Tolstoy's War and Peace *to the mathematics underpinning a Johann Sebastian Bach composition or a Leonardo Da Vinci painting, the integration is so seamless as to be almost invisible. By adopting an integrated services model, the team at PPSS sought to take advantage of natural connections between various disciplines, but also to extend and deepen them; to make the integration purposeful, thorough and harmonious. Each teacher or therapist, no matter how talented, should not be working in isolation; instead, teachers' and therapists' instruction and guidance should be totally woven together.*

The integrated nature of teaching and therapy occurs in myriad ways throughout the day. Teachers are trained to employ certain therapy techniques in their classrooms. Therapists work with staff outside the classroom, including at the pool. And therapists and teachers work in tandem in the classroom on a specific goal or goals. These effective approaches are demonstrated below.

~~~~~~~~~~

In practice: The importance of water

'Good morning!' teacher Margie Lauchland calls out in a cheery voice as another teacher, Chris Edmonds, knocks at the door. 'Thanks for coming to help us with the lunch rush. Would you be able to get Danielle's syringe from over by the sink, please?'

Margie then turns to help spoon yoghurt into the mouth of a girl sitting at the table next to her. Margie and teaching assistant Craig Osborne are assisting half-a-dozen five- to eight-year-old students who are eating lunch. Margie and Craig need extra support because these students are all functionally non-verbal. They either have profound autism or complex and/or profound syndromes, which include intellectual, and often physical, disabilities. Consequently, many of these children have special dietary requirements.

'How much today?' Chris asks as she picks up a syringe.

'100 mL.'

As Chris goes to fill the syringe, Margie's attention is caught by another boy who rises from the table and, with a twisting, stiff-hipped gait, takes two deliberate steps towards the toilets. He then collapses into a heap and the teaching assistant helps lift him to his feet again.

'Great walking,' Craig says.

'Would you look at that!' Margie exclaims to Chris.

'Excellent!' Chris smiles.

Margie and Chris share an impromptu consultation. 'I find if you seat the students at a table, just as you would at home, they are naturally prompted to do what we want them to do,' Margie explains.

'He's looking really good,' Chris responds, as she positions herself in a chair behind Danielle, who remains seated at the table. Chris reaches around Danielle and presses the plunger so that a few drops dribble into her mouth. The eight-year-old girl pushes back, shaking her head, and appears to be having difficulty swallowing even though the syringe isn't filled with a foul-tasting medicine, but simply with water.

'Good work, Danielle,' Chris encourages the child, for whom this is clearly hard work.

Danielle was born without a swallow reflex. For the past 18 months, her PPSS team has been working on teaching her how to drink.

'In this room, it's important to be clever about what goals we set for our students, because it takes them such a long time to master a new skill,' Margie explains. 'In Danielle's case, swallowing was the top priority because it's a vital skill—we have to be able to drink. Our bodies need water! And there's an extra benefit—she's has gained strength in the muscles in her face and she's learning how to smile.' Margie grins as Danielle demonstrates. 'Some people only see the challenges of working in special education; I've learned to appreciate the smallest of gains, which bring immense rewards for everyone involved with the child.'

Margie has a special affinity for children for whom life is harder than it should be. Her own son has autism. 'I knew I didn't want to teach a class made up exclusively of children with autism—that's what I experience when I go home,' Margie says candidly. 'In fact, when I first came to work at PPSS, I wasn't sure I wanted to work in this room—it seemed too difficult. But now I love it. This is really teaching in its purest form. What does this child really need? Why? How can I help them? It might be three years before something we teach bears fruit, but it's so rewarding when it does. I learn as much about myself from the children as they do from me.'

As Chris leaves for her break, Margie collects a pile of clean tea towels and sits down on the floor next to a girl who is rocking back and forth, babbling to herself and turning the pages in a picture book.

'Time to do some folding, Kate!' Margie announces to the girl, who barely acknowledges her presence. As Margie smooths the linen, she explains, 'I try to make this classroom feel like a home. Most of the skills we are teaching here are designed to help these children in their own homes, with their families.'

Not only will the students be happier, but their families' lives will be improved if these children can learn self-soothing strategies so they can sleep; if they can take themselves to the toilet; if they behave reasonably well and eat without making a huge mess.

'We want our students to be happy, productive little people who can amuse themselves and play on their own some of the time. It was only a few weeks ago that Kate couldn't tolerate me sitting this close to her. This is something we practise. And her ability to tolerate me here sitting next to her marks real progress,' Margie says.

★★★

Another little boy has scooted across the floor to an upright piano. He grabs the keys, pulls himself to a standing position and then bangs with his fist on the keys.

'Good job, Rex,' Margie says, as she plays a few keys in answer. Like many of the staff, she is a musician as well as a teacher. Rex hits a few more notes and then looks up at her in a clear request that she continue their musical conversation. She skilfully segues into a soothing, complex arrangement of 'Twinkle, Twinkle, Little Star'. Then it's Rex's turn again. He plays a few more notes, then drops to the floor to crawl across to an interesting ball. The exchange is a part of the school's intensive interaction program, where staff members 'speak' with the student in whatever 'language' they are using. For non-verbal students, this could be through noise-making, creating vibrations, music or through touch. Staff members help the student learn the functional conventions of conversation through their interaction, such as turn-taking, eye contact or responding to or initiating a meaningful exchange.

Meanwhile, Jacob is back from the toilet. He has an extremely short attention span and moves between activities quickly. He decides he wants a go at the piano and hauls himself up. After plinking a few notes and not obtaining the sensory feedback he was seeking, he moves on to an alternative and proceeds to spit towards the light.

'No,' Margie says, in a clear firm voice. 'No spitting.'

Jacob drops to the floor and starts to seek strong sensory input by banging his head on the floor. Margie drops to the floor beside Jacob and begins to apply deep pressure, concentrating on the boy's shoulders, then his hips to give strong, calming feedback to him.

'I've learned how to give deep-pressure massage from Skye Purtill, our occupational therapist,' Margie explains. 'Many of our children have strong sensory needs and seek feedback from undesirable sources. For one child it might be spitting, for another banging their head on the ground or perhaps playing with their snot or some other delightful way to amuse themselves! The reality is these children crave sensory stimulation and it's really just about finding socially acceptable alternatives. I spent hours perfecting a recipe for fake snot. No, I'm not kidding! Children are looking for the sensation of playing with something gooey. So I make something that's delightfully yucky but that tastes bad, so they aren't tempted to eat it. By playing with the goo, we can encourage them not to pick their noses to self-stimulate.'

★★★

The support that Margie has had from Skye to deal with an issue like pronounced sensory needs is typical of the way an integrated services model works. A well-trained occupational therapist is the person best qualified to assess and diagnose whether a child has a sensory processing disorder. Skye works in collaboration with the student's teacher and family to assess and meet the student's sensory needs. This may include altering the classroom environment by introducing specific stimuli, equipment and activities that meet the child's sensory needs; having the classroom teacher use therapy techniques; or working one-on-one to facilitate sensory experiences with the student. Children with sensory processing disorder tend to have low arousal levels and are sensory seeking or to have high arousal levels and are defensive and can quickly escalate into sensory overload. In either case, the student struggles to interpret information received from their various senses and over- or under-responds to sensory triggers in the environment. For example, while a typically developing child might hear a loud noise and cover her ears, a child with sensory processing disorder (high arousal) might hear the same noise and have a tantrum, withdraw or begin flapping her arms.

Sensory processing is the primal and instant response of a human being to information received through one or more of our senses. Some kinds of sensory input are obvious: we all know that we receive information through what we see, hear, touch, taste and smell. But there are two other senses that are less well known and appreciated. Our proprioceptive sense is linked to sensory receptors located in our joints. Those 'proprioceptors' respond to deep-pressure input, which explains why so many people enjoy a good massage. We also have a vestibular system, located deep in the inner ear, which gives us our sense of balance and helps us know where we are spatially, even if our eyes are closed. It is stimulated by movement.

An assessment is necessary to determine if a student's actions are a result of poor sensory processing or should be considered to be behaviours, which are conscious, even planned, responses to a trigger or situation. Careful assessment by a trained observer is crucial to distinguish between behavioural issues and sensory processing disorder.

If it is determined that a student has a disorder, Skye tailors an individual program for the student called a sensory diet. It may involve changes in the student's environment, as well special activities or the use of specially designed tools and toys. Examples include brushing the student's skin with a special brush, or giving the student deep-pressure massage, as well as perhaps encouraging the student to jump on a trampoline; roll on a physio ball; run in straight lines; use a treadmill or exercise bike; wear weighted belts and vests; chew on specially tailored items; or hold spiky toys or specially crafted weights, many of which are designed in the shape of animals to be child-friendly.

***

Not only has Margie become skilled at addressing her students' sensory needs, but she also has a broad understanding of communication.

The Picture Exchange Communication System (PECS) is a widely used and well-regarded tool for helping children with language difficulties to communicate (Hart & Banda 2010; Magiati & Howlin 2003; Sulzer-Azaroff et al. 2009). It would be difficult to overstate how ubiquitous and versatile PECS is at PPSS. PECS is used throughout the day, whether it's giving a visual schedule of events for the day, spelling out the choices of songs in morning circle, or breaking down large processes into small steps. As an example, 'Brush your teeth' might sound like a simple instruction, but for children who need more details that instruction is broken down into a sequence like this: put toothpaste on the brush; brush bottom teeth; brush top teeth; rinse mouth with water; and wash hands.

PECS can use actual objects or laminated cards, each with a drawing or photograph of an object, place, action or person. The cards are usually attached to a board with double-sided tape. As an activity is completed, that picture is removed and placed in a box labelled 'Finished'.

PPSS also used key word signing. As opposed to Auslan, which is sign language for the deaf, key word signing is sign language for people who hear but can't communicate effectively with verbal language (Grove & Walker 1990; Iacono & Johnson 2004). Only the most important words in a sentence are shown with signs. Many people fear that teaching a hearing child sign language will delay the child's speech. Research by Goodwyn et al. (2000) shows that is not the case, as long as the child is spoken to at the same time. Sign is an easier form of communication than speech and a great way to show children the power and possibilities that exist when they try to communicate.

'While there is very little speech in this room, these children are communicating all the time,' Margie says. 'We use PECS, of course, and key word signing, but much of the communication here is more subtle than that. It's part of the intensive interaction program.'

The theory behind intensive interaction is that all children need to communicate, even if there is an underlying reason why they can't produce sounds or words (Barber 2008; Kellett 2004; Samuel et al. 2008; Watson & Knight 1991). For these children, communication is difficult. For them to want to try, they need to know they are being understood. That means teachers like Margie need to be first-class observers.

Following the communication in this classroom is a bit like searching for flora and fauna in a desert. At first, it appears there is nothing to see. But wait and watch and a hidden world emerges. It is clear that a child's glance may convey fury or delight, that a gesture may reveal hunger or happiness and that a push may signify unwillingness, enthusiasm or a powerful desire for self-control.

'With Jacob, I've worked on catching his eye, so that I can understand him,' Margie says. 'Like a lot of our students, he has vision problems. Helping him learn to track, or follow us with his eyes, helps him engage and be part of the group. That's deeply comforting for children, for all of us, to feel included. We are social creatures. It's a human need and my work is about respecting and encouraging that.'

Margie bends down and encourages Jacob to crawl onto a large, shallow wooden tray, approximately two metres long, one metre wide, four centimetres deep and strong enough for the boy to lie on. As Jacob puts his face against the wood, Margie gently bangs on a wooden frame near his feet and he visibly relaxes. 'This is a resonance board, through which Jacob feels the strong vibrations and sounds. Jacob is a child with high sensory needs, who needs strong sensory input to be able to process or make sense of the signals he is receiving. Because he's not making full use of his vision, he seeks sound and vibrations as primary stimuli. By engaging with him through his preferences, we have a chance to observe his behaviour when he is engaged and understand which need is being met through the engagement.'

But, there are huge physical demands that go with working with these children—especially as they get older, larger, heavier and stronger.

'I've been working in this class for three years,' Margie acknowledges. 'I have developed tendonitis and my body is tired. It doesn't matter how careful you are. I love these children, but this will be my last year in this room. I need to be in a class where I teach standing up.

'But I'm in no hurry to leave the school, not a chance! I love the freedom I have to teach through the arts. That's what makes us human, the desire to express ourselves, and it's so important for all children to have that opportunity.'

★★★

From the classroom, we follow the class to the pool. The look on Jacob's face is serene. He stretches out his arms to paddle, then cups the water, revelling in the drops that fall from his fingers. His eyes show his delight.

'Good work, Jacob,' smiles physiotherapist Janet Hutchinson.

It is difficult to believe this calm, relaxed boy is the same boy who was banging his head on the floor in Margie's class. According to Janet, to say that Jacob loves the water is an understatement.

'Outside the water, Jacob often chooses to lie flat on the ground because it's hard for him to know where he is in space. He's getting closer to walking independently, but he doesn't quite have it worked out yet because of problems with balance and orientation in space. This work in the pool helps him integrate his body with his mind,' Janet explains.

'Good job, keep paddling,' encourages swimming instructor Anna Pawlowski, who oversees the class and works individually with students. Anna is wearing her third pair of bathers for the day. It's too cold to change back into wet bathers and she has back-to-back classes. The class sizes vary depending on the ability of the students. For students who are less able, there is a ratio of 1:1 of students per staff member; for students who are the most able, the ratio is 2:1. All classes have a spotter out of the water watching the entire class and the students are always within an arm's length and never out of sight.

Anna turns her focus to another boy, who is wearing his bathers but is still in his wheelchair and hasn't entered the water yet. A student occupational therapist points out to Anna a tube sticking out of the boy's abdomen. The boy has just had a percutaneous endoscopic gastrostomy tube (PEG) implanted in his stomach because he isn't able to eat enough food to supply him with the calories he needs. Anna still wants him to swim. The student occupational therapist, physiotherapist and swimming instructor have a discussion about how best to deal with this situation. After the collaboration, Anna dashes over to the office for bandages and tape, and carefully covers the PEG with a waterproof bandage. The others watch her careful work and agree he is okay to enter the water.

'This is our first year of offering this kind of hydrotherapy class,' Anna explains. 'Skye and I took a workshop taught by Janet Styer-Acevedo— she's the guru of hydrotherapy in America.' Anna and occupational therapist Skye Purtill now have certificates in Neuro-Developmental Treatment-Based Therapeutic Aquatics for Paediatrics.

'Janet Styer-Acevedo told us her work in the US with her private patients has shown that you get the greatest improvement when you do an intensive hydrotherapy program, rather than just teaching children once a week. After we took the class, Skye and I changed our therapy classes. This year, at the start of all terms, we do one intensive week of daily, 50-minute lessons with the children who need this the most,' Anna explains. During the rest of the year, these students also get one or two sessions per week of hydrotherapy.

'This is very exciting for me. I am a physical education teacher. In the pool helping me work with the students are physiotherapists, occupational therapists, teaching assistants and student teachers. That's because this is a one-on-one class,' Anna says.

'We put the intensive therapy session at the beginning of the term, right after the holidays, because that is when children are fresh and rested,' adds Skye.

This student is concentrating greatly while she explores the use of paint and art utensils which support literacy learning: writing and mark making. She is developing her grasp: from a palmar grasp to a finer grasp.

Drama techniques can help students to engage with the world around them while supporting their understanding and interpretations.

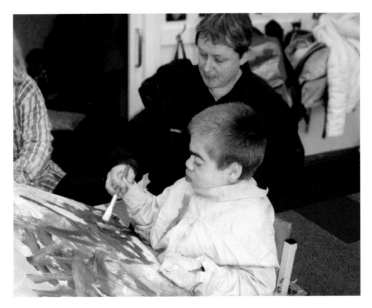

Students are supported to engage with learning through the richness of visual arts and the use of colour, texture and movement.

During Art Therapy different media is used to support students to express feelings and understanding of the world around them. This student is making figurines to represent her family.

Through dance, children learn spacial awareness and
mathematical concepts such as up, down and around.

This student draws his perception of the world using
colour and form.

A Class Act performance.

This student shows the confidence to perform individually, displaying his own style of dancing.

The confidence to perform in front of a live audience is evident when students put on their costume and stage make up. This is the culmination of a year's learning.

Literacy through role playing develops communication and language – both verbal and non-verbal.

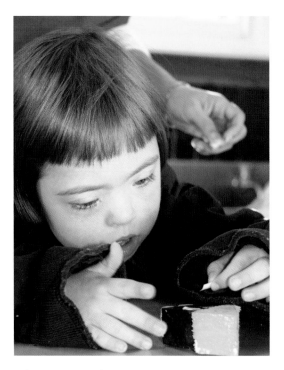

Demonstration of fine-motor skills using blocks and paper to create a little house. Mathematical concepts of shape and colour are addressed.

As the child holds the flower, she paints her interpretation. After being provided with three colours she matched accordingly.

Fine motor and numeracy skills are developed as children play.

Finding what motivates and engages students – bubbles!

Dance provides an opportunity to develop a range of curriculum areas such as dressing skills within a meaningful context.

Daily living skills are regularly practised within a real-life context located on-site, called the House of Independence (donated by Thiess).

Cutting, measuring, stirring and food preparation are important skills to learn for future life.

Following a sequence such as a recipe to prepare food enables students to be more independent.

Music provides a range of experiences not only in sound production but interaction, performance, confidence, leadership, communicating emotions and, for some students, the beginning of language development.

The arts allow adults and students to share meaningful interactions. Bella Irlicht joins in a music session.

Music therapy involves interaction, exploration and enjoyment. For some students music can physically relax them and centre their emotions.

Drums are a simple instrument utilised for learning to copy and sequence, performing individually or as part of a group, following a beat or, for some students, to provide sensory stimulation or feedback.

For students who need additional language support, a range of communication techniques are used in collaboration with the speech therapist.

Camps provide a range of alternative educational experiences while developing independence, social skills and a break for mum and dad.

Students become confident in the water while attending to their physical health needs.

The on-site pool provides opportunity for hydrotherapy, sensory processing programs, physiotherapy, water familiarisation and swimming. This also provides a real-life context for practising dressing skills.

The daily activity of the Health Hustle keeps all school members, students and staff, fit and healthy. It also offers an opportunity for gross motor development for students with specific goals. This is a fantastic start to the day as people chat on their journey.

Gross motor coordination is developed through activities that support children in social and leisure contexts.

Students enjoy playing a variety of sports, developing communication, gross motor skill, eye–hand coordination and leisure skills.

Bike riding is a much loved activity that not only develops gross motor skills but expands social and leisure skills too.

The Short Break Cafe! An extensive menu ensures students develop skills in food preparation, health and safety, safe food handling, waiting on tables and money management. This highly prized program also provides sustenance for staff and visitors.

Working together to identify plants for a recipe develops friendships, social skills and community ownership.

As the boy with the PEG is shifted into a water-proof wheelchair and gently rolled down the ramp into the shallow end of the water, Anna turns to help Rex, who has changed and is ready to come into the water. 'We've learned in past sessions that Rex doesn't like the water at first, but he gets used to it,' Anna explains.

She holds Rex's hands and gently leads him towards the ramp. But as his toes touch the water, his face lights up. He walks forward, gaining confidence. As the water level deepens and he is better supported, Rex lets go of one of Anna's hands and soon is only holding one finger of the other. 'He couldn't do this last year!' Anna says, smiling.

In the background, soft gentle music plays, as if the setting is a romantic restaurant rather than a busy pool. 'We use quiet music for hydrotherapy. For our regular swimming classes, we use bouncier tunes. Songs the children can sing, such as "London Bridge" or "Six Little Sausages in the Pan". Humpty Dumpty falling off the wall is a great way to get children into the pool. We work on whatever their classroom goals are—speech, counting, living skills through getting dressed. But for hydrotherapy, we want them calm and relaxed.'

An allied health assistant on placement from RMIT University named Angelo is helping another boy. He holds one end of a kickboard while the boy holds the other.

'Angelo, let go of the board,' Anna chides gently. 'He has to do it on his own.'

'I'm scared he's going to fall over!' Angelo objects.

'Keep him in waist-deep water. That gives him support. If the water is too shallow, it's difficult.'

Anna is working with eight-year-old Gina. As Gina stands in the water, which is up to her chest, Anna uses a boogie board to make waves in the water. The motion of the water does not topple Gina, who smiles with delight. On land, Gina uses a walker. But an intensive program, which includes physiotherapy as well as hydrotherapy, has made massive improvements.

'At the beginning of the year, Gina could not stand in the water by herself at all. Not for even two seconds. She would fall over. So we started working with her in water up to her neck and she held onto the railing. Gradually, slowly, we moved towards the more shallow end,' explains

Anna. 'And now, months later, she can walk in water up to her chest for 20 minutes by herself!'

The improvements transfer to dry land. Gina is gradually learning to take some steps without her walker. She can now walk from the school to the park—a distance of 500 metres—just holding the hand of a staff member.

The beauty of hydrotherapy, Skye explains, is that it provides physical input, but without the cumbersome restriction of gravity. Consequently, children are able to accomplish movements that would be difficult or impossible out of the water. Once a skill has been mastered, a student is often able to replicate the new skill, or something close to it, on land.

'The results of this hydrotherapy have been amazing,' Anna explains. 'This is our first year, so we're just beginning to collect the statistics, but overall what we have found is that the students make improvements in balance, coordination and even walking.' She pauses, surveys the calm, peaceful scene. 'But I think the greatest benefit of all is just how it makes them feel.'

★★★

It is December, time for the school's end-of-year performances. The junior, middle and senior schools each hold separate productions, comprised of individual class acts. There are five classes in the junior school and each presents its own performance, united by this year's theme of Up, Up and Away.

Like the other classes, Margie Lauchland's class has been rehearsing for months. While each class act is unique, all include performances that are choreographed and carefully tailored to the students' abilities and desires. Children and teachers make the costumes, props and scenery. They experiment with makeup, choose the songs and dance moves, tinker with lighting, tweak, rehearse and practise some more. PPSS prides itself on having productions that are spectacular enough to impress any audience.

But each class act is much more than a lavish stage extravaganza: it's a way to showcase to families, friends and PPSS staff how far these students have come and how much they have learned during the year.

To the strains of 'Why Walk When You Can Fly?', the students of Margie's class, assisted by a few teachers and assistants, take to the stage. As the music soars, an assembly of bees zig and zag, a ladybird dazzles with scarlet plumage and the wings of an enormous sapphire butterfly gently flutter. The skills these children demonstrate are remarkable and bear witness to their progress: being able to dance with someone else; tolerating the noise and stimulation of a production; flashing a brilliant, hard-won smile; executing dexterous steps and pivots with a walker; and grasping and throwing brightly coloured balls.

The spotlight finds Jacob, whose gold and black bee stripes shimmer. He holds tightly to a teacher assistant. Across the stage, Margie crouches, stretches out her arms and beckons to Jacob. And then it happens. Jacob releases the assistant's anchoring hands and catapults forward in a daring, headlong solo flight. Not one or two steps this time, but a pell-mell dash across the stage. Thanks in part to those intensive hydrotherapy sessions, in part to work in the classroom, and most of all because of his own keen desire and readiness, this determined, eight-year-old boy is now walking. He is one of two boys in this class who have learned to walk this year. Jacob's smile says there is no turning back. As he reaches his destination, the audience erupts in applause.

~~~~~~~~~~

As opposed to the one-to-one therapy sessions, a therapist may observe an entire class to see if there are ways to improve a particular therapy for all students in the class. One of the most important goals for every student is communication. It is vital for children to be able to make their thoughts, feelings and desires known, whether they are verbal or not.

~~~~~~~~~~

In practice: Team-teaching children on the autism spectrum

PPSS speech–language pathologist Anne Schwarz makes her way to the peppercorn playground, which takes its name from the shady tree in the corner. She's here to work with teacher Clare Duncan, art therapist Anita Bragge and some middle-school students for an hour-long personal development session. These students have been grouped together to address their particular communication goals.

Originally, this class was held inside; however, most of these students are on the autism spectrum and are movement seekers. The team thought they might have more success working on communication goals if they did so in an environment the students enjoyed. Anita has not brought any art materials, but rather is on hand to assist Clare, as well as to understand more about communication strategies used in the school to ensure she is consistent with other staff when working with students outside of therapy activities.

The students are excited to exercise outside, but to do so they must first exercise their communication skills. Jonah stands in front of Anita, who holds up a large laminated sheet. It contains photographs of a swing, a bicycle, a trampoline and several other pieces of equipment. The sheet is a form of choice-making. Photos are used instead of picture symbols because every student in this class can understand what these photos represent.

Looking directly into Jonah's eyes, Anita points to one of the photos on the sheet and asks, 'Would you like the swing?' She points to another. 'Or a ball?' She waves to indicate the entire sheet. 'What would you like to do?'

Jonah jabs at the sheet.

'All right then, trampoline. Good choice.'

As he strolls towards the trampoline in the centre of the playground, Anne asks Anita, 'Did Jonah pick the trampoline last week, too?'

Anita nods. 'He loves the trampoline.'

Anne looks down at a clipboard in front of her, flips to a page regarding the boy. 'I really like how you two are documenting these sessions,' she says. 'From what you've recorded, it looks like he's actually picked the trampoline every single time! Do we think that's a conscious choice or could he be selecting "trampoline" because of where the photo is located on the sheet?'

'We thought about that,' says Clare. 'So we made a new sheet. We moved the photo but he still picks the trampoline.'

'Great!' nods Anne, making a note for herself.

Meanwhile, another child, Harry, is now standing beside the trampoline. Clare holds out her hand, palm angled down, using the key word sign to reinforce her verbal 'Wait.' Harry pauses. Clare continues, 'Jonah is using the trampoline. Then it's your turn.'

'Did Harry use the photos?' asks Anne.

'No. But he came over to the trampoline. That seemed pretty clear.'

Anne nods. 'I still think we need to get Harry to use the photos. Can you see if he makes the same choice using the photos?'

Clare dutifully shows her laminated set of photos to Harry, who looks perplexed. He points expectantly at the *real* trampoline beside him.

'Yes, Harry, I understand,' Clare persists, 'but which of these *photos* do you want?'

The boy reluctantly surveys the sheet and chooses the correct photograph. Communication can be hard work.

Anne knows it must seem strange that she insists Harry uses a photo, when he was clearly communicating without it. 'Parents often ask me the same thing: "Why do we need to use pictures when we know what our daughter wants?" But not everyone understands a child with a speech difficulty as well as the family does! And you can't always point to the thing or activity you want. Let's say Harry had been inside, wanting to use the trampoline, but we didn't understand him? That's frustrating for a child and can cause them to stop trying to communicate. That's where pictures come in.'

Anita returns to the picnic table, which is serving as Anne's de facto office. She has a question regarding another student, who is on the autism spectrum. 'Gemma is still on the swing. What's our communication goal? Should I encourage her to get off, look at the photos again and choose something else?'

Anne ponders. 'You could.' She scans her clipboard. 'But judging from the notes you've made, she'll probably just choose the swing again.'

Anita nods, relieved. 'That's what I thought, but I wasn't sure.'

Now it's Clare's turn to visit the picnic table. 'I have a question about Tristan. He doesn't seem to like any of the choices we've given him.'

'What *does* he like?' asks Anne.

The team thinks.

'Playing with his shadow,' observes Anita.

'And air guitar,' nods Clare. 'He loves seeing his shadow play air guitar.'

'Could we take a picture of him playing air guitar and put that on his photo sheet?' asks Anita.

'He might like that,' agrees Clare.

'Let's give it a try,' Anne agrees. 'I think we have to keep remembering that our goal is to give them every opportunity to communicate. If we find something Tristan wants to do, he's more likely to make an effort to communicate his choice.'

Clare agrees. 'You know, I relate to these children. I was always a visual learner in school. Pictures help.' Clare surveys the students on the playground, who all seem engaged and calm. 'Doing things they like motivates our students. I think we do better when we focus on things that are interests-based rather than straight outcomes-based. We hide the work under something that is fun. They learn the same things, but it's easier for them to focus and achieve. And success brings confidence!

'I've found that many of these students can really only pay attention to a task for 10 to 20 minutes at a time; then they need a break. Now that they've had an opportunity to jump and swing, they should be ready to sit and concentrate,' she says.

Clare has also worked with occupational therapist Skye Purtill, who has brought various materials into the classroom to help the students when getting outside isn't an option.

'Some of our children bounce on a mini-trampoline before they tackle a challenging task,' Clare says. 'Or there's the gym ball to roll on. During circle time, one of our children holds a hot water bottle filled with cold water and another boy holds a large weighted toy that is shaped like a gecko. The sensory stimulation helps them to concentrate. What I've learned from Skye is that if we help the children to regulate their sensory modulation we are more successful in engaging them in learning.'

Anne nods. 'I like collaborating, too. When I sit in on a class, I see how my communication strategies actually work—or don't. I also can help problem solve and figure out other ways of fostering speech and communication. I try to work with all the teachers to make sure their rooms are set up so that speech therapy occurs naturally throughout the day, whether they are in swimming with Anna, doing art with Ross, a dance class with Cathy, or in class with Clare! We try to teach, wherever we are, whatever we are doing. That's the nature of the integrated curriculum.'

~~~~~~~~~

When children need extra assistance with a particular therapy, a therapist may spend time one-on-one with them in a classroom. The goal is that this therapy session will be integrated into the classroom activity. Integration also occurs when skills worked on in the classroom are amplified or extended through students' work with a specialist teacher. The following two situations—involving a speech therapist and a music teacher—provide snapshots of a few of the many ways in which learning is integrated, across disciplines, and throughout the day, at PPSS.

Such integration should seem natural and organic as is demonstrated when speech pathologist Anne Schwarz spends time working one-on-one with a transition student named Jenny. The pair has a 'conversation' about the popular television series, The Simpsons. *Yet Jenny doesn't say a word. The smiling teenager has galactosaemia disorder. Jenny can wave, smile and nod her head, but she cannot talk. Jenny's powerful desire to communicate has been assisted through a special tool called a MightyMo.*

In practice: Silent 'talk'

'Who's that, Jenny?' Anne asks Jenny.

Jenny looks down at a communication device in front of her wheelchair. With rapid movements she presses several squares until a picture of a blue-haired lady pops up. She presses the picture and a voice says clearly, 'Marge.'

'That's right! And who else is in the show?'

Jenny taps another picture on the screen and the same voice says, 'Krusty the Clown.'

For Jenny, the MightyMo communication device is a great tool for chatting with speech therapist Anne Schwarz about popular culture. But it's also far more significant. The device is crucial because it enables Jenny to tell those around her not only what she knows, but what she wants and needs, as well as how she is feeling.

'Jenny is such a happy, sunny person—she's always smiling. We aren't always sure if a nod means "Yes, that is what I want," or if she is just nodding to please us, because she has an agreeable nature. Now we can teach her to ask questions and make statements. She can say things like, "Come here," as well as "Go away!" That's a lot of power and independence,' Anne explains.

'See here?' Anne points to some of the pictures, which show a pegboard, bubbles, photos, a shopping game, even nail polish. 'I'm adding her own vocabulary, in addition to a vocabulary that comes factory installed, with things she likes to do. Much more motivating! And I make sure to include verbs like cut, paint or bake, in addition to nouns like paper, picture and cake. That way Jenny will learn to make sentences and have a real conversation. We teach her how to use the device by modelling.'

Anne looks at Jenny, who is deeply absorbed in her MightyMo. 'This tool isn't for everyone. It takes a certain level of cognition, which Jenny has. She's also a very social and engaging girl. This device is giving Jenny a voice,' Anne says.

The MightyMo cost about $6000 and was applied for through the Victorian state government's Aids and Equipment Program. The device is an older model, and once, after another student chewed through its power cord, it took three months for a replacement cable to be shipped from the manufacturer. Jenny had to do without her MightyMo for nearly a term. But Jenny is making up for lost time and Anne is impressed by how quickly she has mastered her version of Facebook: the page with her friends' names on it.

Although Anne does spend some one-on-one time with Jenny, she also appreciates the power of the integrated services approach. 'I do targeted individual sessions with particular children who need a specialised therapy, like Jenny. An allied health assistant also works with her for two 40-minute sessions each week in a one-on-one setting, using the device to communicate with her, model its use and providing Jenny with opportunities to use it to communicate. But much of my time is spent in the larger classroom setting. Most of these children won't have someone working one-on-one with them always. It's not realistic. My job is to work with all the teachers to make sure the children are getting as much speech therapy input as possible.'

Anne's conversation is interrupted by laughter. Another child at the table has just cracked perhaps the oldest joke in the world—she's squished her hand under her armpit, becoming a human whoopee cushion. Jenny is laughing as loudly as everyone else.

Anne giggles, then points to Jenny's MightyMo and says, 'I have something to say!' Jenny watches intently as Anne 'says' her remark on the device. She pushes a button and a picture of a funny face appears. 'That was silly!' the voice says.

Jenny nods, giggles and presses a button with a smile.

★★★

PPSS is a school with plenty of horns, bells and whistles. That is both figuratively and literally true. In the music room, children can plunder a box filled with tinkling bells, maracas, even a train whistle. There are also two pianos, a guitar, keyboards, microphones and amplifiers. In the exercise playground there are balls, bicycles, monkey bars and trampolines. The school has a wardrobe closet full of costumes and props, outside are vegie gardens bursting with produce, the gym has state-of-the-art physiotherapy equipment, and students have access to art supplies, audio-visual equipment for making movies, and a variety of kinds of computers. PPSS is extremely well equipped with a wide range of items that have been bought, donated or acquired.

Significantly, children like 15-year-old Lachlan come into contact with a wide variety of these items every day, in one class or another.

At 10 am on a typical Monday, he and the other children in Sarah Haji's transition class can be found in music class, taught by Margie Lauchland, who became the school's music teacher in 2011. The class is working on a traditional song called 'I Hear Thunder'. The teenagers will make the sound of the thunder with African drums. The drums are nearly a metre tall, with a slender, hourglass-shaped, hollow wooden base.

'Make sure to lift the drum off the ground when you play it,' teacher Margie Lauchland explains. 'That way you get the vibrations and the best sound.'

Lachlan carefully experiments with his drum, then gives it a bang. With a smile of delight, he follows Margie's directions as she alternates between loud and soft, fast and slow, making thunder and rain, in keeping with the song:

> I hear thunder, I hear thunder,
> So do you, so do you,
> Pitter patter raindrops, pitter patter raindrops,
> I'm wet through, so are you.

The lyrics are displayed on an easel in front of the children; another page contains the musical notation.

'We have literacy with the words of the song we are singing,' Margie explains later. 'Numeracy comes from the counting—holding a beat for four counts, for example. We also learn opposites—fast, slow, high, low. There's memorisation. Singing works on breath control. And we are also teaching the children to take cues from one another—to be part of a group, not just in their own world. Some children, like Lachlan, like music so much, they've joined in our choir.'

Recently, during a school assembly for Remembrance Day, Lachlan and the other students sang 'Advance Australia Fair'.

'I believe there are three songs every child in Australia needs to know, because they are sung in public. The first is the national anthem. The second is "Happy Birthday". And the third? That's the song for their footy team!' Margie says.

After music it's time for recess, and Lachlan heads straight for the exercise yard, where there is a range of equipment to choose from. Grabbing a basketball, he and a couple of other students practise their jump shots. In between, Lachlan works on some tricks, including trying to roll the ball back and forth along his forearm. He's so coordinated that during bicycle education, he rides a typical bike, rather than the large, three-wheeled variety many children at the school use. Lachlan, who has Down syndrome, shows no sign of the fact that he had two holes in his heart at birth and needed surgery.

Later, back in the classroom, the students work on Australian currency. They are learning the denominations of bills, and must distinguish between the various gold and silver coins. To make the lesson more intriguing, classroom teacher Sarah Haji employs a range of software on an iPad®.

As Lachlan watches in utter absorption, a voice says, 'Pick out the 50 cent coins.' When Lachlan makes the correct selections, a panda on the screen roars its approval.

'Perfect!' crows Sarah, 'You guys are getting too good at this.'

From African drums to iPads®—from the ancient to the up-to-date—the tools are used to engage, inspire and educate students.

Chapter 5
Integrated Services Committee

∙∙∙

Keeping everything running smoothly at Port Phillip Specialist School is no easy task: coordinating the work of the many therapists, specialists and teachers; responding to day-to-day needs; navigating through crises; and, importantly, monitoring student progress.

The Victorian state government mandates that every child in special education must have an Individual Education Plan (also sometimes referred to as an Individual Learning Plan). In many schools, developing and monitoring these plans is primarily the job of the classroom teacher, in conjunction with a student's family, perhaps with guidance from the principal. But during her tenure as principal, Bella Irlicht thought there was a better way.

To oversee all the students and ensure each child got the most out of his or her education, Bella created the Integrated Services Committee. But this committee isn't just interested in education. Committee members consider the whole child. How is the student's health? How is her emotional and social wellbeing? How are her parents and siblings? Bella knew that for all children, but especially those with special needs, education does not happen in isolation. This is no cloistered ivory tower, set apart from the 'real' world.

The job of the Integrated Services Committee is prioritising, coordinating programs, ensuring teams are collaborating, and ensuring accountability for resources and student progress. If a student has lost his way, how best to get him back on track? If he has exceeded the goals in his plan, what should he strive for next? If a family is in trouble, how to best get that family assistance immediately? The committee holds meetings at least twice a week, but also calls emergency sessions if requested by a teacher or parent. The committee is considered so fundamental to PPSS that it has been called 'the heartbeat of the school'.

~~~~~~~~~~

The heartbeat of the school

Carl Parsons

The Integrated Services Committee ensures that every student's individualised plan is reviewed regularly. Ros Jennings, the school's social worker, and I, as director of integrated services, share the roles of organising and running the meetings. Ros and I listen to the issues brought to us by various staff members before the meetings. We advise staff members to have discussions with other relevant staff; for example, Ros and I might recommend that a teacher have a discussion with the psychologist about a behaviour a particular student is showing; or we might recommend that a staff member who has an interest in a particular program should devise a blueprint for how the new program might be offered at the school and present it to the Integrated Services Committee.

The committee consists of all the senior leadership team staff (principal, assistant principals and team leaders), classroom and specialist teachers, teacher assistants, relevant therapists, psychologists and social workers. The exact make-up of the committee fluctuates depending on what is being discussed. If a particular topic or group of students is being discussed, then relevant teachers, therapists and specialists are invited to attend and participate in the discussion. Often the idea of the meeting is to get the viewpoints of various people to help solve problems. Once there is a consensus, then the committee can allocate staff to put in place appropriate procedures to resolve the issue.

Any staff member who has a concern about a student's program can attend the review. The committee provides a forum for the multidisciplinary team to discuss any issues that have been identified, seek clarification and ensure that appropriate services are delivered. The committee might recommend home visits, assessments, trial therapy sessions, additional consultations with other professionals outside the school, interaction with hospital staff, pursuit of equipment for a student's home, and additions or changes in programs. The committee reviews each student's need for programs. For example, not every student can be involved in the intensive hydrotherapy program due to the high staff-to-student ratios required, and because the relatively small size of the pool limits large groups of students from being involved at one time. Thus, the committee might have to determine, with input from all relevant staff, which students might be included each term for the intensive hydrotherapy program. Frequently, the school examines ways to support families in crisis—this may include organising meals to be prepared for a family, respite care for a child with a disability, or counselling for a sibling of a student with a disability. In some cases, the school has agreed to liaise with funding bodies to arrange for equipment to be used at home for children with severe disabilities. The committee can also identify areas of need within the school or for families. The committee recommends and assists in planning programs and training for parents, siblings and grandparents.

In order to ensure that the integrated service delivery model is working, the school has a number of review mechanisms. Teachers and therapists are required to collaborate on all school reports. These reports include oral presentations to the Integrated Services Committee about students. This is how the committee learns about particular issues that might need attention to improve student learning. The team members must also collaborate on written school reports to families that occur twice per year—one at the end of Term 2 and the other at the end of the school year in Term 4. These reports are based on individual progress in goals in cognitive, affective and psychomotor domains (that is, intellectual development, interests and values, and physical skills). Finally, the school maintains ongoing professional development for staff to continue to learn about integrated service delivery. Professional development is geared towards keeping our staff at the cutting edge in understanding students with additional needs.

PPSS has taken up the challenge of meeting the comprehensive needs of students with disabilities through a unique integrated service delivery model. This model of service delivery is still evolving at the school. Staff believe that integrated services are an appropriate and innovative way to improve outcomes for students, even though there are ongoing challenges. Ongoing 'evidence-based practice' research will help to identify the benefits to students. The school is currently engaged in research that will help PPSS evaluate the benefits of this model and the improved outcomes for students.

Watching the Integrated Services Committee at work is a bit like watching an educational version of the TV medical drama House; *a teacher presents a case study of each of his or her students to a team of colleagues for peer review. Ideas and suggestions are considered and a plan of action is formulated and enacted. The team meetings are chaired by Ros or Carl and attended by all senior staff, including principal Robert Newall. The meetings run for no longer than an hour and Ros and Carl set an agenda and determine which additional teachers or therapists should be present. The following meeting is typical, although on this day Ros had a conflicting meeting, so Carl served a number or roles, as the group's facilitator, note-taker and chair of the meeting.*

In practice: Taking the pulse of PPSS

The school day has just finished when the members of the Integrated Services Committee file into the conference room and take their places around the large oval table. The meeting is formatted so that each child's progress is mapped in several key areas: education; behaviour; social and emotional performance; and any relevant changes in the family and life outside PPSS. Today it is Justine's turn to review the progress of the students in the class she teaches, who are all teenagers, and discuss issues that may have arisen since the last review of the particular students.

'I'd like to start with James, if I can,' says Justine. 'He is really having some problems. Recently, we find that noises are just sending him off. We're also having real difficulties getting him to go anywhere outside of the classroom with anyone.'

Art therapist Anita Bragge interjects. 'Would it help ease the transition to my session if I brought my materials to your classroom and we did our work there instead of going to the art therapy room?'

'That could be interesting as a way of meeting his continuing needs,' someone agrees.

'Still, we can't do that for everything,' principal Robert Newall adds, to prompt more discussion of how to solve the problem.

'If we cut out all transitions, then he will never leave the classroom,' agrees Justine.

'How long has this resistance been going on?' Carl asks.

'He seems to have gone downhill over the last two months.' Justine pauses, considering. Then an idea dawns. 'Actually, it's really been since our student teacher left. Before that, James transitioned willingly.'

Everyone nods. A change in teaching personnel can be a major adjustment for any student, especially a student with additional needs who struggles to cope with changes in routine.

In this case, the boy struggling with the departure of a student teacher has severe autism. Social problems associated with autism sometimes lead to difficulties with transition. Now that the team better understands the catalyst for James' escalating behaviour problem, Carl probes for a solution.

'Have you tried a visual schedule?' Carl suggests.

A visual schedule is a set of pictures that communicates a series of activities or the steps of a specific activity. They are meant to communicate clear expectations for the student and allow the student to predict upcoming events. In this way, visual schedules help students understand and manage the daily events in their lives.

'We have tried these but he refuses to use them—I suspect he feels he is not in control,' Justine explains.

'Have we done a sensory assessment?' Carl asks.

Assessment by a trained observer might reveal that a student has difficulties processing sensory information about the environment and from within his own body (from his senses of sight, sound, touch, smell, taste, balance and proprioception).

'There isn't one in his electronic file.'

Carl makes a note, and suggests the school's occupational therapist Skye Purtill should conduct a sensory assessment.

'We'll have Skye take a look,' Carl says. 'Meantime, let's see if we can introduce some strategies to help him. We need you to keep track of his meltdowns, try to identify what triggers them, then try to prevent them.'

Carl suggests that Ros, as the social worker, and Marg Gawler, the psychologist, could help Justine with strategies to examine James' behaviour.

Justine nods. 'I did speak to Ros earlier this year, after James intentionally stomped on my foot. It made me nervous. I don't want to be hurt. Ros was really helpful. She said not to force James to do things he's not enjoying, because it just doesn't work and it's hard on me as a teacher. We have to make compromises that keep us safe, but also use the things James likes to do to engage him more in being prepared to transition to other environments,' Justine says.

'Exactly,' Carl says. 'You need to be safe. And we need to do a better job of figuring out what James *does* enjoy. Then we teach from there.'

Justine considers. 'The only thing he really likes is being left alone.' The team waits to see if Justine can think of anything else. 'He also likes building. Sitting quietly with building blocks and constructing elaborate towers.'

'That's a start,' Carl says. Carl's mantra is 'Hate the behaviour, never the child.' When a student is struggling and acting out, it is his belief that there is a reason for the behaviour. The task is to address the cause of the behaviour. But it's also crucial to identify the student's strength or interest, which can become the foundation upon which the student can build and grow.

Sometimes teachers need assistance finding that talent or remembering it in the day-to-day program in the classroom. A team approach provides support, generates ideas and solves problems.

'James also likes the health hustle first thing in the morning,' adds Ned, another teacher who knows James. 'He always participates in that.'

Carl nods. 'We need to offer James opportunities to participate in more things that he likes that are outside the classroom,' he suggests.

'What are his goals?' asks Rob, the principal.

Like every student at the school, James has three main goals that have been established in a state-mandated student support group meeting attended by a team comprised of the teacher, the therapy team and the child's parents. Originally, PPSS created a list of seven goals per student, but decided it was unproductive to focus on so many.

Justine explains. 'We are trying to encourage James to be more tolerant of social situations. That's a big goal for his parents. One goal is for him to say hello to several staff each day.'

'He says hello to me!' Carl says. Then adds. 'But then again, I'm not requiring him to do anything.'

'Does a "high five" count?' asks Georgie, the music therapist.

'I think so,' nods Carl. 'Regardless, I think we have to be mindful that we are dealing with a child who is solitary by nature. Being gregarious is hard work for him. We might need to discuss altering these goals.'

Justine makes a note.

'What would you say your primary goal is for James?' Carl asks her.

Justine considers. 'My honest goal is to have him calm and not to have the violent outburst each day, which is physically and emotionally dangerous for him and everyone around him. His dad says these explosions also happen at home.'

'How do we make it happen?' Carl asks the group.

Art therapist Anita interjects again. 'I've got some room in my schedule. I am happy to do some one-on-one art therapy sessions with James. Once he trusts the situation and is more relaxed we can work to help him adapt to transitions.'

Carl agrees. 'I think more one-on-one with several of our specialists would be very beneficial for James. Good, we're making a plan that we can begin to help him move from his room and help Justine with the difficult behaviours.'

Carl revisits all that has been discussed and a number of people make notes on which to follow up.

'Now, which student is next?' asks Carl.

The committee listens as Justine continues to give progress reports concerning the rest of her students. There are triumphs, including significant improvements in numeracy and communications, for a number of students. One girl has become highly motivated to read, thanks to her interest in the *Twilight* series; another boy's numeracy has improved since he's begun using an iPad®. Medical issues also get a great deal of attention. One boy is quite heavy, although he barely eats. Could he have a thyroid problem? Justine should touch base with the family with the support of the therapy team or the psychologist. Another boy who suffers selective mutism—he speaks at home, but never at school—has made enormous progress controlling occasional outbursts of temper. Everything seems to be on track for him.

But Justine has one student who she's not quite sure is in the right place.

'As you know, Etienne was attending his local mainstream school, but he was having limited success in school work and in making friends. His mum decided that PPSS may be a better option for him, but he says he feels stupid to be here,' Justine says. 'In a way, I don't blame him. I mean, it's a massive change to suddenly be sent to a special school at his age. He's frustrated and angry. And I would say that while he can't read or do maths like a typical boy his age, he is capable. How can we find opportunities for him to work, using his machinery skills?'

The team discusses the matter. Are there some trade classes nearby? Perhaps he should attend a different class at the school? Or should he attend a different school altogether? When should the changes occur and how should they be handled, to avoid adding further insult to a teenage boy who is already struggling with self-esteem? Plans emerge for looking into alternatives for Etienne to develop self-esteem and to excite him about education.

But just as the meeting is about to break up, another topic arises. It's one reason for these meetings—the way potential problems can be shared, when the group gets together.

'Does anyone else have a concern about our kids being on Facebook?' asks speech–language pathologist Anne Schwarz.

'Tell us about your concerns,' Rob says.

'Actually, I've seen some of our students on Facebook, too,' Ned adds.

Rob is now paying close attention.

'I don't know if you have seen Adam's profile,' Anne continues, 'but he's written down that he is at a technical college, rather than saying he attends here! Obviously, he thinks that looks cooler. Some of our students are pretty street smart, but they are also vulnerable and I worry about them being preyed upon by the wrong people.'

'Luckily our students tell us what's going on,' Ned says.

'Oh, I suspect they share about 80 per cent,' Rob says. 'The trouble is the other 20 per cent is probably the really worrisome bit. We need to address this.'

'Maybe a class on computer safety?' suggests someone, as others chime in. Perhaps an article on students and social networking should be sent home via the newsletter to raise awareness for the parents also.

'These sound like good ideas,' Rob agrees. 'I know Ros is dealing with this, but I'll also talk to the transition teachers about it. We'll get right on it.' He looks up at the clock. It's nearly 5 pm. 'All right, thanks everybody.'

The session is over. There will be another meeting later in the week for committee, but it's home time for now.

~~~~~~

While each student is reviewed at least once a year by the committee and concerns can be raised at the committee meetings, if a teacher, therapist or parent has a specific concern about a child, an emergency meeting can be called. For families, this is one of the most important services offered by the school. That's because for them, a concern about their child isn't just academic. Sometimes problems seem to snowball, until the carers feel like they are about to crash.

~~~~~~~~~~

In practice: Open-heart surgery

Lauren and John sit side by side outside the PPSS conference room. Lauren flips through a magazine she clearly isn't reading and crosses and recrosses her legs. John has retreated into his mobile phone and fires off a blizzard of texts. The door to the conference room opens. 'Are you ready?' asks Ros Jennings, the PPSS social worker. The couple exchanges a look that indicates they are as prepared as anyone can be for what feels like open-heart surgery. Even though they requested this meeting with the school, it is still distressing to attend, because being here is an open acknowledgement that they have no idea how to improve the behaviour of their seven-year-old son. Recently his behaviour has been so antisocial and occasionally repellent that talking about it—even to an empathetic audience—is painful.

Lauren and John know they are not alone. They realise that there are other parents of children with an intellectual disability for whom the child's behaviour is far more difficult to accept than the fact that he or she struggles to master certain concepts and skills. The knowledge offers little comfort. To be here is to admit how bad things are and how defeated they feel.

They slouch into the conference room and take seats opposite one another at a large oval table. In addition to Ros, psychologists Marg Gawler and Sarah Wright are there, as well as the director of integrated services, Carl Parsons, Early Education Program teacher Yvonne Miller and art therapist Anita Bragge. PPSS principal Rob Newall and vice-principal Alison Druce are not able to be at the emergency meeting today.

'Thanks for coming back in again to meet with us about Jeffrey,' says Carl. 'First, we'd like to ask you what you see as the more recent problems with Jeffrey. Then we can tell you what we have observed.'

Lauren clears her throat. 'As you know, our son has been particularly challenging recently. We've been back to the neurologist, who is tinkering with Jeffrey's medicine, but she says behaviour problems are just an element of his genetic disorder. He is impulsive—we think there are problems in his frontal lobe—and he has been hitting and kicking, and so many tantrums! His big sister is the number one target, which is a huge issue, especially since Jeffrey is now seven. He's a big boy.'

John picks up the thread. 'We'd been told a special diet might help his behaviour and saw an expert at an autism clinic, but the results were disastrous.'

Lauren interrupts. 'I blame myself. We were told to eliminate carbohydrates, sugar, dairy and gluten, but not given a lot of guidance about what Jeffrey *could* eat. He developed shocking diarrhoea and that's when he started smearing faeces in the playground here. I cannot begin to tell you how mortified we are.'

Carl nods, puts down his pen. 'There's no need to be embarrassed. We've seen smearing before.'

Lauren feels a surge of relief. She'd feared their son was the only child to act out in such a way. She shoots a quick, hopeful look at John, who returns a cautious smile.

Ros nods in agreement. 'That said, we do need to make sure it stops. Regardless of the reason, this behaviour is antisocial and it's one that can escalate. The diarrhoea is the trigger, but it isn't the cause. We believe that this is an attention-seeking behaviour. Often the best way to eliminate such a behaviour is to deny a child the attention he craves. That can work with swear words, for example. But in this case, that's not possible. Smearing is a health risk. We can't ignore it. We cannot have faeces on the playground equipment.'

Lauren's relief fades. She puts a hand to her hair. She cleans Jeffrey's uniform, takes pride in his tidy appearance. It is how she was raised. How she has tried to raise her son. She is so sick of talking about, dealing with and living with shit. Someone hands her a tissue.

Everyone is silent as she pulls herself together, as she tries to shove aside the painful images of her beautiful baby boy before he was like this, when he was full of smiles and confidence. Even his comfort with strangers now worries her, since he has no concept of 'stranger danger'. Don't go there, don't think about the future, one day at a time, that's what the experts say; advice far easier to impart than to follow.

Lauren wants to ask, 'Why? What happened? What's wrong with his brain that he would do this?' Or, more truthfully, 'Why does our son, *my* son, do this?' When Jeffrey throws food all over a store, bangs his head on the floor, hits someone simply because they walk by, or screams as if she's beaten him when she takes him to the bathroom, she tries to remain calm and composed, avoiding the gaze of even the most sympathetic stranger, because her son's behaviour devastates and isolates her. It's hard not to think that it is her fault. Because she's his mum.

John speaks the fear that is stuck in the back of her throat. 'You know, I used to just think, well, this is bad, but it will get better. Things will improve. But recently, I've found myself wondering, what if things stay the same? Or get worse?'

Carl is all business. All information. 'What we know about intellectual disability is that behaviour often goes in a wave pattern.' He demonstrates with his hand marking peaks and troughs in the air. 'There are good times and bad. Over time, we hope that those mountains become hills, the canyons turn into valleys and everything evens out for him and you. But, regardless, the way to proceed is to plot a course and be consistent. We'll make a behaviour management plan and stick with it, through the good and the bad.'

'It gives you something to hold on to,' Yvonne offers.

'And you don't have to do this on your own, remember,' Ros adds. 'We have targeted challenging behaviours before and had good success.'

Lauren and John nod slowly. They do remember. Somehow they have just lost their way.

Carl clears his throat. 'Let's address the smearing first. I've spoken to our therapists, and they recommend that you send Jeffrey to school wearing an all-in-one garment. So there is limited access, so to speak.'

'Is he still on the diet?' asks Yvonne.

John snorts, 'No. We got rid of that quack.'

'How is Jeffrey at home?' asks one of the psychologists.

'He's not smearing. But he's really tricky with his big sister. If she doesn't pay attention to him, he kicks and hits her,' Lauren responds.

'How do you respond?'

'Time out. It works some of the time. But now our daughter just ignores him—even when he is being absolutely lovely, which does happen. I tell her, "I understand how mad Jeffrey makes you, but when your little brother does something good, you need to praise him!"'

Marg Gawler, a psychologist, speaks up. 'Actually, you need to stop that.'

'Pardon?' Lauren responds, shocked.

'You need to stop telling your daughter how to feel and how to behave with Jeffrey.'

Lauren is clearly indignant. 'But the other day, Jeffrey sang a beautiful song to Matilda, sang her good morning and she ignored him!'

Ros leans forward. Her level gaze bores in on Lauren. 'Do you have siblings?'

'Two brothers and a sister.'

'Did you fight as children?'

Lauren hesitates. She can see where this is going. 'Of course we did.'

'And how do you get along now?'

'But that's diff–'

Ros puts up her hand. Her eyes are full of an equal measure of understanding and firmness. 'If you want Matilda to grow up despising her little brother, by all means keep doing exactly as you are doing. But if you would like for her to accept him, to be kind to him, to understand this difficult situation, then I encourage you to let her work this out on her own. Kids are entitled to a range of feelings, just as we adults are. I'm sure Jeffrey makes you mad, too,' Ros says.

Marg chimes in. 'Every bit of research shows that siblings of children with a disability are more empathetic, more caring, more nurturing than their peers,' she says. 'But they have their own anger and sorrow. This is a loss for them, too. Remember, your daughter is only 11. This is a difficult road, for everyone in the family. You need to give her the space to work it out, on her own. Then I suspect you will find she will develop a fine relationship with her brother. Many of the teachers at our school have siblings with special needs. I've met Matilda—she's a lovely girl. And despite these recent problems, Jeffrey is a lovely boy.'

Lauren hears the words, but, right now, it is difficult to believe that her son is a lovely boy.

John jumps in. 'It seems like whenever we get a handle on one bad habit—like screaming—he just substitutes it with something else! It drives us crazy. I want to yell, like I would at a typical son, but I try not to.'

Ros looks at John with an affirming smile. 'I'm so glad you *don't* yell, because it doesn't work. Neither does smacking, as all of us will tell you. Those strategies actually make the situation much worse, because they give

Jeffrey attention, which he craves. Never mind if it's negative attention—he has engaged you and that's what he craves,' Ros explains.

'We do know how upsetting and infuriating some of these behaviours can be,' offers psychologist Sarah Wright. 'Do you have some respite? Anyone who can help you take care of your son?'

'We're okay,' Lauren says.

'Let us know if you need more help. You need breaks,' Ros adds.

Yvonne jumps in. 'Regarding discipline, Jeffrey needs clear guidelines,' she says. 'You're right that "time out" doesn't always work. If possible, the best reinforcement relates to cause and effect. Remember, you can use some of the techniques we have talked about before. If Jeffrey throws something, instead of giving it straight back to him, remove it for a minute or so before returning it with an explanation of what is expected when he is given the toy or food back. If Jeffrey is spitting food, remove him from the table for a minute, before trying again.'

'Do you know about ABC?' Carl asks.

Clearly this isn't a question about the alphabet, so Lauren and John shake their heads.

'B is the behaviour,' Carl explains. 'Every behaviour—even a socially repelling one, like smearing—has a purpose.'

'The best way to get rid of a negative behaviour is to change either A or C,' Ros explains further.

'A stands for antecedent—whatever happened just before the negative behaviour—and C stands for consequence. If Jeffrey hits his sister, then A is what happened just before. Perhaps he'd been enjoying time just with you. The consequence, C, is what happens immediately after that behaviour—his big sister leaves, and Jeffrey gets you all to himself. In that case, the best response might be to say "No hitting, Jeffrey," then lavish attention on Matilda,' Ros says.

Lauren sits up and leans forward. 'Can I ask about another example? When we put Jeffrey to bed at night, he bangs his head on the door. I can't leave him because he will really hurt himself. What do I do?'

Carl nods. 'Well, the A in that situation is going to bed. The B is the head banging. What is C?'

Lauren and John look mystified.

'Actually, C is that Mum or Dad comes!' Yvonne says. 'Jeffrey has gotten exactly what he wants. We tend to think of consequences as being synonymous with punishment, but a consequence is *whatever happens as a result of the behaviour*. For Jeffrey, the fact that you come back is a reward.'

'So what are we supposed to do?' asks John, whose exasperation has now been replaced by interest. He had hoped this session would be a catharsis for his wife, but suddenly realises this is also a strategy session. John likes puzzles and excels at motivating employees. But it has been infinitely harder to know how to encourage his endearing but infuriating son. Jeffrey can't be fired or shipped off to boot camp if he underperforms. This all comes back to his brain. Lauren and John both know that. They just don't know how to work around the issues. Sometimes to Lauren it feels like there is a roadblock inside Jeffrey's brain and teaching him is like trying to find a new path through a dense and unfamiliar forest without a map.

The team brainstorms. Yvonne says, 'I would suggest that in order to change this behaviour, you stand right by the door. As soon as Jeffrey climbs out of bed, pop him right back in. It may take 100 times the first night or so. Don't look at him or speak to him. If you talk he's …'

'… getting attention. I see,' replies Lauren.

'How long does it take to fix a bad behaviour?' asks John.

'28 days,' someone says.

'That long!' Lauren exclaims.

Carl nods, then says, 'Let me put it another way. It might take your typically developing daughter four or five times to change a behaviour—'

'More like 10 times!' John snorts.

Carl laughs. 'That's because she's almost a pre-teen. But guess how many times you must be consistent to get your message across to a child with an intellectual disability?'

'Twenty?' John guesses.

'Try 400 or more,' says Carl.

John groans.

'Four hundred times of doing exactly the same thing,' Ros adds cheerfully.

Carl nods. 'If you give up after 50, Jeffrey knows he has beaten you. So think about your strategy first. And then don't give up.'

Yvonne looks over at the parents, who are beginning to look hopeful. There seem to be solutions—or at least strategies—for the challenging and baffling behaviours of their adored seven-year-old son.

'Lauren, John, how are the two of you?' asks Marg.

John nods. All good.

Lauren agrees. 'We are lucky there.'

'That's good,' the Marg says. She doesn't quote the statistic that up to 80 per cent of couples who have a child with a disability divorce. Lauren knows that one off by heart. 'The two of you need to have a date night, every week,' she says, as if rattling off a prescription.

Lauren smiles, as John interjects. 'Has my wife been in your ear about this?' But he is smiling for the first time during the session.

He then turns and looks directly at Carl. 'So Jeffrey isn't going to get kicked out of school?'

Carl actually laughs. 'Kicked out? Of course not! These are the problems our students face. This is a specialist school. It isn't easy to be a parent at the best of times.'

Yvonne smiles and pokes John, who is sitting next to her. 'But next time, don't wait so long. It's important that behaviours that are worrying are addressed early so they don't become insurmountable.'

These parents are seen regularly at the school; they will be watched carefully by the team from the meeting and chatted with frequently, as Jeffrey is monitored for changes in his behaviour by his teachers, the therapy team and the psychologists. The meeting over, Lauren and John are overwhelmed by relief and feel more reassured and supported than they have for weeks.

Chapter 6
Visual and Performing Arts Curriculum

···

The Victorian Essential Learning Standards (VELS) is the Prep to Year 10 curriculum for all Victorian schools, including special schools. Port Phillip Specialist School employs a Visual and Performing Arts Curriculum (VPAC) to achieve many of the goals outlined in VELS.

VPAC does not train students to become actors, dancers or artists. Instead, it uses the visual and performing arts to teach students to think, to communicate and to live fuller, richer lives.

The desire for this novel curriculum came from Bella Irlicht's frustration at seeing her students sitting at tables, trying to learn in essentially the same way as mainstream children were learning. She was convinced PPSS students learned things differently and, consequently, would learn more if taught through the arts. She wanted to give them that opportunity.

VPAC is unique to PPSS, but it shouldn't be. VPAC could and should be used in special schools across Australia and throughout the world. It also could be adapted for use in mainstream classrooms.

~~~~~~~~~

Drawn to the arts: PPSS and VPAC
Carl Parsons

By 2003, then PPSS principal Bella Irlicht had the fully-serviced school's talented staff of teachers, therapists and specialists working in concert using the integrated services model. But she wasn't convinced students were achieving their full potential. Was there a better curriculum to teach them? Some teachers and therapists were experimenting with new ideas, many involving one or more of the dramatic and performing arts. Was it possible to use the arts in some more structured, thoughtful way? And if so, how?

After observing numerous classes and interviewing staff about student progress, Bella believed the school's curriculum was due for an overhaul. The staff members were asked to reflect upon PPSS's students' abilities and strengths. What did the students like doing the most? What did they not like? What strategies helped them learn? What interfered most with their learning? Over the course of a year and many discussions about the curriculum, the school staff identified that many students struggled with a traditional educational curriculum. The staff identified that some students had a lack of motivation, lack of attention, poor motor skills, sensory-avoidance or -seeking behaviours that interfered with learning, problems with memory and problems with learning to use language, speech, reading, writing and maths. Students did not have the ability to sit and listen for even brief periods of time and did not enjoy passive learning. Thus, many students could not access a traditional curriculum based on text or oral language skills. Indeed, many of our students had already 'learned' by the time they came to PPSS that they could not do many tasks like their aged-matched peers who did not have special learning needs. Many showed active resistance and lacked motivation to participate in activities that they had previously found extremely difficult. And yet like all specialist schools, PPSS was expected to follow what was in essence an adapted version of the mainstream curriculum—the Victorian Essential Learning Standards (VELS).

VELS was developed for mainstream students and many aspects did not relate to students with disabilities. One of the curriculum areas in VELS, for example, was 'speaking and listening'. It was assumed that when students came to school (at five years of age) they could start to give presentations in show-and-tell activities and could begin to listen to stories read by the teacher. But many of our students with special needs can't sit up or sit still for more than five seconds. Many have never spoken. The VELS curriculum placed a great emphasis on interacting with others in the classroom, including during play activities, and having discussions about important topics. Unfortunately the nature of the intellectual disabilities in special schools means that many of our students can't even answer simple questions, much less have a discussion.

Many of our students have difficulty interacting with others. Indeed, for many of our students, we focus on getting them to learn to put on clothing, brush their teeth, go to the toilet, wash their hands or participate in a group activity. For many of our students with autism, the focus has been to get them to be able to move from one classroom to the next without having a tantrum or meltdown. The VELS curriculum did not reflect this. What it recommended to be taught was fine, for students who had average intellectual capability; our students did not. The Victorian state government revised the curriculum in 2009 and 2010, particularly focusing on the curriculum for students who have difficulty learning. This new aspect of the curriculum is known as VELS Working Towards Level 1—and it is designed for students who do not have the ability to do VELS in their first year of school. Working Towards Level 1 provides a framework to assist students with intellectual disabilities work towards being able to participate in VELS, but it recognises that many students with intellectual disabilities may never be able to progress beyond Level 1.

Reflecting on the curriculum

Staff reflected on activities that motivated, engaged or calmed our students, activities that our students seemed to enjoy or assisted their learning, as well as the skills our students had learned. As staff began to compile lists based on their reflections, a pattern began to emerge.

We found that a small number of students (some with autism spectrum disorders) had perfect pitch and loved to sing. Many of these students would sing songs using words that were not used in daily interactions. Some would smile in recognition of familiar tunes. They would often spontaneously begin singing at various times throughout the day. Some of these students would request music to be played by bringing CDs to their teacher. We found that another group of students would spontaneously begin dancing when they heard music. Some would spin or demonstrate interesting movements with their bodies. Other students would clap their hands or make sounds for enjoyment. Some would use various objects as instruments to make noise. Some of the students would take turns between listening and making noise using various sticks, shakers and drums. When music was played students would often join in an activity. Some students loved drawing and would repeatedly make detailed pictures. Many others took pride in being able to draw an animal, a building or a favourite cartoon character on their own. Other students were excellent at communicating their needs, wants and emotions through mime and natural gestures.

We also realised that our students learned best by participating in activities that required or encouraged movement. It was noted than many of our students were involved in out-of-school activities, including art, dance, drama, music, aerobics, swimming and a range of sporting activities. Indeed, various disability support groups and local and state governments had initiatives to support people with disabilities becoming involved in extracurricular activities. Many of these activities were motivated by the notion of inclusive communities. More importantly, these activities were enjoyed by our students and many excelled in them.

The staff also began to make lists of a range of new, alternative or popular arts-based remedial and therapeutic activities or programs designed for use with students with disabilities.

Auditory programs listed included:
- auditory bombardment
- auditory integration training, based on the Bérard method
- auditory processing training
- interactive metronome
- lexiphone
- listening fitness
- listening program
- melodic intonation therapy
- modulated music
- Mozart effect
- music therapy
- rhythmic entrainment intervention
- sound therapy
- spectral activated music of optimal natural structure (SAMONAS) method
- therapeutic listening
- Tomatis method.

Movement and sensory programs listed included:
- balance remediation exercise training
- brain gym

- brushing technique, also known as therapeutic brushing or the Wilbarger protocol
- craniosacral therapy
- daily life therapy, also known as the Higashi school
- dance therapy
- deep pressure for sensory processing disorders
- developmental exercise
- educational kinesiology
- feldenkrais
- learning breakthrough (psychomotor) patterning
- manipulative therapy
- martial arts training
- moto-kinaesthetic therapy
- patterning, based on the Doman–Delacato technique
- physiotherapy
- primary movement programs
- qi gong
- reflexology
- reiki
- sensory diets
- sensory integration training
- sensory motor programs
- therapeutic touch
- yoga therapy.

We also began to make a list of teaching techniques and strategies that were already in use at school that helped student learning. These included:

- aided language displays
- bicycle riding
- Children's Aided Language Tools (CHAT) system
- comic strip conversations
- computer-assisted learning
- concept maps
- gestures
- graphic organisers
- Incredible Five-Point Scale
- listening to music, especially favourite songs

- physical prompts and cues
- Picture Exchange Communication System (PECS)
- Pragmatic Organisation Dynamic Display (PODD)
- relaxation music
- sand and water play
- sensory programs
- sign language
- swimming
- trampolining
- video modelling
- visual 'no' or 'off limits' cues
- visual 'something hurts' board
- visual activity checklists
- visual calendars
- visual carry cards
- visual choice-making
- visual circles concepts
- visual classroom rules
- visual contracts
- visual cues and prompts
- visual cues to support language
- visual cues to support speech
- visual daily routine boards
- visual emotions thermometer
- visual first, then boards
- visual interactive language stimulation boards
- visual labelling system
- visual mini-schedules
- visual needs request cards
- visual reinforcement boards
- visual schedules
- visual sequences (events)
- visual shopping lists
- visual situation preparation
- visual social rules
- visual social stories
- visual timers and clocks

- visual trip schedules
- visual work tasks.

Linking curriculum to learning styles

Numerous authors have indicated that there are at least three common learning styles—visual, kinaesthetic and auditory (Carbo et al. 1986; Prigge 2002). Although there are differences of opinion about the exact percentages of people who have the preferred learning styles, it is generally agreed that visual learners are the most frequent. For example, Gangwer (2009) in his book on visual impact and visual teaching, noted that: 65 per cent of the population prefers visual learning; visual information is processed more rapidly in the brain than text; 70 per cent of the information sent to the brain is through visual channels; and 40 per cent of all nerve fibres connected to the brain are linked to the retina. It has also been shown that students with autism spectrum disorders learn best with visual supports (Dettmer et al. 2000; Johnson et al. 2003).

Another large component of learning includes movement and touch. This is called kinaesthetic learning (Stafford & Dunn 1993). Kinaesthetic and tactile learners learn best by touching, manipulating objects and actually doing an activity. It is believed that more boys than girls are kinaesthetic learners. As more males than females have disabilities (Wellcome Trust Sanger Institute 2009), it makes sense to include kinaesthetic learning activities into the daily routine.

Auditory learners are probably the least frequently found types of learners, with some estimates indicating that less than 15 per cent of the population uses auditory learning as their primary mode of learning (Gangwer 2009). Auditory learners do best in listening tasks and activities that involve words.

At PPSS, we knew that many of our students' disabilities meant that they had great difficulty with attending, listening and learning verbal communication. The research supported the idea that using visuals and getting students moving during activities they enjoyed might improve their willingness to participate and engage, and assist their learning of routine tasks, daily living skills and emotional regulation.

With this in mind, the school began to pursue the use of visual and performing arts more fully. As PPSS director of integrated services, I was asked to locate research literature about the use of visual and performing arts to teach. Classroom teachers and specialist staff were asked to systematically evaluate each student's interest and capabilities in using the visual and performing arts. Bella contacted a number of university staff who specialised in the arts and began having discussions with them about the prospect of using the arts for teaching students with disabilities.

All this information was used to make the decision that the school would begin to implement a Visual and Performing Arts Curriculum. Bella brought in education consultant Pam Russell and a team of educational experts in the arts and educational leadership to guide the development of such a curriculum. Rob Newall, now PPSS principal, first came to the school as a member of this team of education specialists.

The team of experts began to work with the staff and the state government on plans to implement the Visual and Performing Arts Curriculum. Senior staff members in the Victorian Department of Education were consulted. The department was interested and felt that since there was no formal special education curriculum at the time, the school could proceed.

Although the school had some art-related specialists, it began to employ additional art educators to fill positions as art, dance, drama and music teachers and therapists. These staff members helped to build our new curriculum.

Meanwhile, we continued to explore the literature about using visual and performing arts with students with specialist needs. Much of the previous work had focused on using the arts to teach typically developing students, although some work focused on teaching students who came from 'disadvantaged' backgrounds. Some of the published work alluded to the potential advantages of using visual and performing arts with other populations including 'the disabled'. Some of the research referred to Howard Gardner's work on multiple intelligences.

Gardner proposed a theory of multiple intelligences, suggesting that people possess at least seven different forms of intelligence (Gardner 1985, 1993, 1999; Gardner & Hatch 1989). The theory posits that distinct thought processes exist in separate sections of the brain. Gardner points out that students have individual strengths in each area and if we can uncover each student's strength or preferred mode of learning, then we can exploit the skills in their preferred style area to help them learn. Gardner claimed these differences 'challenge an educational system that assumes that everyone can learn the same materials in the same way' (1985, p. 83). His system proposed that everyone learns differently.

Each of the intelligences or learning styles are, in general, characterised by core components, such as sensitivity to the sounds, rhythms and meanings of words, and capacities to discern and respond appropriately to the moods, temperaments, motivations and desires of other people:

1 Visual–spatial learners think in terms of physical space. They have an excellent visual awareness and perception of the environment. They are good at creating and manipulating mental images, and at orienting their bodies in physical space. They like to draw, do jigsaw puzzles, read maps and daydream, developing pictures in their minds. They enjoy activities that require them to do spatial tasks and use visual imagery and visual imagination. Teaching tools include using physical models, graphics, charts, photographs, drawings and 3D models on the computer. They also learn from watching television and working with multimedia.

2 Bodily–kinaesthetic learners use the body effectively. They have a keen sense of body awareness. They like movement, making things and touching things. They communicate well through body language and can be taught through physical activity, hands-on learning, acting out and role-playing. They enjoy using tools, equipment and real objects.

3 Musical–rhythmic learners show sensitivity to rhythm and sound. They love music, but they are also sensitive to sounds in their environments. They may study better with music in the background. They can be taught by turning lessons into lyrics, speaking rhythmically and tapping out time. They enjoy activities that involve listening to or using musical instruments.

4 Interpersonal learners enjoy understanding and interacting with others. These students learn through interaction. They have many friends, empathy for others and social awareness. They can be taught through group activities, seminars and dialogues. These students enjoy interacting and talking with other people. They are social and enjoy activities where they can socialise.

5 Intrapersonal learners tend to be self-aware. They know what they like and don't like; they know what they are good at and not good at. They are in tune with their inner feelings; they have wisdom, intuition and

motivation, as well as a strong will, confidence and opinions. These students tend to shy away from others. They like time on their own to reflect on their lives and interests.

6 Verbal–linguistic learners use words and language effectively. These learners have highly developed auditory skills and often think in words. They like reading, playing word games, making up poetry or stories. They can be taught by encouraging them to say and see words, and they enjoy being read to by an adult or teacher. These students enjoy computers, games, multimedia, books, tape recorders, written messages and lectures.

7 Logical–mathematical learners love to use reason and calculation. They think conceptually and abstractly and are able to see and explore patterns and relationships. They like to experiment, solve puzzles and ask questions about space and the galaxy surrounding earth. They can be taught through logic games, investigations and mysteries. They need to learn and form the big concepts before they can deal with details.

Gardner's theory provided us with a useful framework to help us understand some of our students' learning preferences and styles. We recognised that many of our students had real strengths in the kinaesthetic and rhythmic areas. The majority of our students had problems related to the verbal–linguistic areas. Thus, Gardner's theory helped us to recognise that our students at PPSS would more likely learn by using their interests and strengths in visual and performing arts, rather than through activities which relied on linguistic skills, in which most students had weaknesses.

We also reviewed Lev Vygotsky's work on mediation, dialectical learning, scaffolding, the zone of proximal development and a social–cognition learning model. Vygotsky (1962) proposed the concepts of the zone of proximal development and scaffolding. The zone of proximal development is the gap between what a student can do independently and what he or she can do with support. Scaffolding is the support provided to help a student learn something new.

Vygotsky pointed out that learning takes place only when the activity being taught is just slightly more difficult than previously experienced or learned. If the activity or task is too hard or outside the zone of proximal development or if the teacher or peer uses tools that are too advanced for the learner, it is likely that the learner will experience frustration or a feeling of failure. Thus, teaching should ensure that a learner can be successful while mastering new skills, by gradually and slightly increasing the difficulty of each task.

Vygotsky also believed that learning occurred through a combination of playing and working. Using the learner's abilities and interests facilitates learning through interacting during fun or preferred activities. He points out that collaboration in actual concrete activities with an adult or slightly more capable peer facilitates learning. The adult or peer provides scaffolding that includes assistance with planning, organising, doing or reflecting on the specific task being learned.

Scaffolding makes it easier for the learner to undertake a task successfully. This sort of strategic support expands the possible learning experiences and increases the rate the learning can be achieved. Scaffolding extends what is possible for a learner to perform and thus expands the zone of proximal development. The provision of educational support by a teacher or slightly more able peer can enable higher-order problems to be solved and more learning to take place.

~~~~~~~~~

One reason Bella believed it was vital to have special education teachers, therapists and specialists employ an arts-based curriculum at PPSS is that the arts are essentially non-verbal and many children with an intellectual disability have little or no speech. Music, dance, art and drama offer different ways to reach a child other than words. Any artist, musician or performer will tell you that the visual and performing arts are languages of their own. Being granted access to the languages of the visual and performing arts, and to the new opportunities for expression these new languages allow, can be a profound experience for children who struggle with traditional forms of communication.

~~~~~~~~~

In practice: The Rubik's Cube® principle

Among students requiring special education, the fastest growing category of disability is autism spectrum disorders (Rutter 2005). The Australian Advisory Board on Autism Spectrum Disorders (MacDermott et al. 2007) reported that on average across Australia, one in every 160 children is diagnosed with autism spectrum disorder. Approximately 75 per cent of those diagnosed will be males. There is beginning to be recognition that more girls may also have autism, but they may not be diagnosed as easily as they show a different profile to boys (Hartley & Sikora 2009). Nearly 40 per cent of the students at PPSS are on the spectrum. With this in mind, Bella asked Early Education Program teacher Simone Boness to develop a school manual on autism spectrum disorder. The manual is filled with ideas and strategies for the parents of these students.

The arts-based curriculum works well for children on the spectrum, as well as for other students at the school, regardless of their disability, because the arts are multifaceted and infinitely adaptable. If a child doesn't learn his or her numbers by drawing them in the sand, perhaps singing or drumming them is the answer. If learning about the planets seems humdrum, what about making them out of papier-mâché? Practising to get dressed is much more interesting if a student is pretending to be Buzz Lightyear or Alice in Wonderland. A student can forget how hard it is to stretch tight hamstrings or Archilles tendons when learning how to moonwalk like Michael Jackson. With a performing arts curriculum, there is a point of entry for any student.

Take, for example, the junior-school class taught by Kristy Parks. Her class of five- to eight-year-old students includes children with a wide range of disabilities, personalities and learning styles.

'You can read an abundance of information about a particular impairment but not truly appreciate the unique characteristics and different learning styles from one child to another with the same impairment,' Kristy explains. 'The arts provide an outlet for each child to express his or her distinct personality. Children learn through different means and the multiple intelligences of children just fascinate me.'

In her class, Kristy sees particular learning styles emerging. 'While we use all forms of the arts as tools to teach communication, numeracy and living skills, it is evident that some children learn best and express their understanding better through one particular art form over another. For example, with learning the skills required to brush their teeth, Janice learns best through singing songs about teeth brushing, while Paula prefers to role-play and model her teacher and peers as they brush their teeth. Then there is Jake, who learns best from the shared reading of big books followed by the drawing of pictures to consolidate this new information.

Through the umbrella of the arts, all children have the opportunity to learn and express themselves in a fun and engaging way.'

All of the children in the group are engaged by music, which explains why Kristy facilitating a vigorous version of the 'Hokey Pokey' today. It not only encourages speech, but dancing gets the children active and using their whole bodies, which is key to helping these children learn. Enthusiasm and the association of words with movement encourages communication.

'Okay,' Kristy pants, breathless, as the children clap. She sticks a small laminated Picture Communication Symbol (PCS) back on the board with double-sided tape. 'Whose turn is it next?' she asks. With his head down, Richard raises his hand, excitedly moving it up and down.

Richard has autism spectrum disorder. He can only say a few words and finds it challenging to make eye contact. He shuffles forward, surveys a selection of PCS that show descriptive pictures above the title of various songs and hands his choice to Kristy with a smile.

'Oh, "Hot Potato"! Good work, Richard!' Kristy beams. As education support worker Michelle Hilder turns on the familiar Wiggles' tune about hot potatoes, cold spaghetti and mashed bananas, Richard rocks back and forth, grinning in delight.

'Now who wants to sing?' Kristy asks. As she does so, she holds two fingers out and together at the side of her mouth, then raises her fingers in a loopy '3' shape finishing near the top of her head to demonstrate singing using key word signing. Kristy explains, 'I use key word signing throughout the day, in addition to verbal language. Key word signing provides me with another tool to communicate with the students.'

For children whose language is just emerging, being misunderstood is a common and frustrating experience. The sound 'ba' might be the noise produced by a sheep, or 'bed' or 'bad'. A child grows increasingly frustrated as he repeats the sound to make himself understood. But if that same child holds his fingertips together while saying 'ba', anyone who understands key word signing will know what he is really asking for is a 'ball'.

Picture Communication Symbols and key word signing are vital tools for many of the children at PPSS. Because PCS provides visual sign-posting, it anchors children in time and place. That can reduce anxiety and frustration. The students know what is going to happen, when it will happen and what they are expected to do. At its best, PCS operates as a visual scaffold, over which key word signing, props and speech are layered so that children are immersed in a communication-rich environment.

Like any Prep teacher, Kristy likes to read to the children from large format story books. The pictures and text are designed for budding readers. As she reads *Rat-a-Tat-Tat* by Jill Eggleton, Kristy is partly focusing on the story of a girl who opens her front door to an unsavoury cast of characters, including a dragon and a crocodile. But Kristy is also working on developing her students' memory, concentration, communication and language skills—helping her students learn how to anticipate, predict and recall events.

She asks parents to do the same when children take their readers home at night. 'I encourage parents to ask lots of questions. What is the boy wearing? Where is he? What's the girl doing? We always want to encourage language and communication, but we also want them to label, categorise, recall and anticipate. The children's other homework assignment is to record what the day's weather was like. That also helps them to learn the days of the week,' Kristy explains. Such daily activities encourage communication at home between parents and children, and provide special time for them to spend together.

At PPSS, the three main areas of focus are communication, numeracy and living skills. And what better way to teach the living skill of getting dressed than a weekly pyjama party? Every Monday, the children in Kristy's class bring pyjamas, combs and toothbrushes to school. They enjoy the humour in pretending to sleep—there are some excellent fake snores. They are encouraged to make a choice of cereal or toast for breakfast. If they pick toast, they can then choose jam or honey as a spread. After eating, students are encouraged to place their dishes in the sink and wipe down their place at the table before brushing their teeth, washing their faces and changing out of their pyjamas and into their school uniforms. Modelling each other is highly effective and in this case it is a key tool in encouraging children to master skills they often find challenging.

Also included in the day are individual programs designed for children who need extra attention. Posted on the wall are activities given by the physiotherapist: Rebecca needs to climb the monkey bars to develop strength in her arms; Julie's assignment is to step between the rungs of a ladder laid on the floor to encourage her to look at her feet; and George needs to stretch his hamstrings. George can do this sitting against a wall or by doing animal walks—pretending to be a bear or a rabbit. The idea is to make hard work fun.

Watching teachers at PPSS is like watching a puzzle whiz complete a Rubik's Cube®. Hungarian sculptor Eno Rubik's square toy has six sides, each comprised of nine squares of the same colour. Since an internal pivot allows each face to move independently, it only takes a couple of quick rotations to turn the puzzle into a jumble of colours. It is difficult for a novice to return the puzzle to its original configuration, even if she has just watched an expert do so, explaining why Rubik originally called his puzzle 'The Magic Cube'. Watching staff at PPSS seamlessly pivot from strategy to strategy, technique to technique, as they strive to bring out the best in each student, is a similar sort of magic—obvious when observed, but not always easy to replicate.

'Last week, we were singing the "goodbye" song and, suddenly, one student who has been very withdrawn popped up and started going around the circle, playing "Duck, Duck, Goose!" It was completely spontaneous. It was the first time all year that he had initiated communication with his peers and we just stopped what we were doing and went with it! Then, there's Mason, who was so shy at the beginning of the year and wouldn't lift his head during morning circle. Role-playing games using binoculars and sunglasses have given him the confidence to look at his peers. He will now hold his head up high during morning circle and smile at his peers without any aids. These special moments ascertain just how powerful the Visual and Performing Arts Curriculum is for these truly amazing children,' Kristy says.

~~~~~~~~~

Many of the teachers at PPSS aren't just special educators, but professional or amateur performers. They love music, art and drama, and choose to perform outside school, which contributes to their classroom performances. Junior-school teacher Susanne Mackey sings in a gospel choir and looks to popular culture for ways to engage the students.

~~~~~~~~~

In practice: Teaching through popular culture

This morning it is morning circle time and Susanne Mackey is singing a 'hello' song. Assistant teacher Kirsten Sharp sits in the circle with the children, her calm presence facilitating the relaxed, attentive mood.

'They weren't always like this!' Susanne admits. 'It took weeks before the students were able to attend to our voices and presence. They also required time to assimilate to being in a new classroom with new routines,' she says.

By now these five- to eight-year-olds know the drill and find the predictable start to the day soothing. Routine is a friend of all children, especially children with additional needs. The musical aspect of morning circle time is engaging and rhythmic, and the props used that symbolise the song choices are made by the class in art sessions with the support of the speech–language pathologist.

Susanne strums her guitar and sings 'What Do You Think My Name Is?' to a girl.

Susanne extends an oversized plastic buzzer and the girl presses a large button. 'Caitlin,' a recorded voice replies for her.

Susanne nods and repeats Caitlin's name, working it into the rest of the song.

While Caitlin uses the buzzer to say good morning, other children wave their hellos using a large, lime-green hand. Susanne looks for eye contact, concentration and the ability to stay connected. The hand helps.

'Holding an object is a way to make an abstract concept concrete,' Susanne explains. 'It's also a symbol, a cue that it is time for morning circle, because that's the only time we use this particular object.

'Most of us are able to pick up on lots of subtle clues to tell us what is going to happen next. But many of these students have autism. Their brains pick up *too* much sensory information. They can't process and integrate it all, and they get overloaded and anxious. So we find ways to let them know what's going to happen next. Order and routine are vital,' she says.

Susanne considers part of her job to be on the lookout for that which delights. Like all the staff at PPSS, she knows that the best way to teach children with additional needs is to start from their strengths—to find their joys, aptitudes and interests, and use them to help a child forward.

'I often refer to Edward De Bono's six thinking hats,' she explains, referring to De Bono's theory of analysing a difficult problem using different kinds of thinking. De Bono symbolises those different styles with coloured hats: white for reasoning; green for creativity; red for emotion; black for critical thinking; yellow for positive thinking; and blue for reflection (De Bono 1985).

Susanne had observed that her students were keenly interested in the *MasterChef* cooking competition on TV. As the season came closer to the finale, the children's interest was piqued and Susanne had a great idea. It was an idea that would require the children to use a variety of those figurative thinking caps. They would also need to put on the tall, white hats and matching aprons she'd bought them.

'I decided we should challenge the other junior-school class to our own version of *MasterChef*,' Susanne says. 'Food is highly motivational!'

The contest was an instant hit. Children brought in recipes from home for simple favourites: toast with jam or honey; fruit skewers; banana bread. Each week, the classes got together to make one recipe, then sample and rate what they'd cooked. The project developed cooking skills, as well as choice-making, turn-taking, numeracy and social skills, in addition to language and communication. But most of all, it was fun.

★★★

Susanne took a roundabout route to PPSS. Her mother had been a principal and teacher at a specialist school, prompting Susanne to fight that option 'with great gusto'. She knew that on a bad day 'poo, snot and vomit can rule your life'. Instead, her desire was to work with gifted children. That was, until she took a course as part of her teaching certificate about working with children with a disability. The professor rocked her world.

'He challenged us. He said you shouldn't be here and you shouldn't work with people with a disability, unless you want not just to be a teacher, but to be an advocate: "What's good for people with disabilities is good for everyone!" That's been my philosophy ever since,' Susanne explains.

'We're not only working with children. We're supporting their families. Families experience all sorts of challenges and there is grief. Many of the milestones typical kids make, these children never will. But there is so much they *do* accomplish. Tremendous things! We explore activities that are creative and fun, but they are also about creative ways to engage a student in their world. We see so much progress,' she says.

As Susanne speaks, there's a glint and sparkle from a swirl of colourful paper fish dancing overhead. The sea creatures, painted by the children, are props for the upcoming school musical. The junior-school students will act in a skit performed to Camille Saint-Saëns' orchestral composition *Aquarium*, from his famous work *The Carnival of the Animals*.

The children love their costumes, which include a dolphin and a starfish. But Genevieve's costume is especially apt. Genevieve has Down syndrome and a hearing impairment significant enough that, at the beginning of the year, the school hadn't listed speech as one of her goals. But Genevieve surprised and delighted them.

'She's not just talking—she's telling the other kids it's morning circle time! She had become very assertive!' Susanne beams.

In the school performance, Genevieve will make her debut dressed as Sandro Botticelli's Venus, emerging from her clam shell.

Through the arts-based curriculum, the students experience a holistic program that supports and engages with each individual child's way of being in the world. The program allows for self-expression that the teachers attune to and then work to build programs that deepen and broaden the students' learning. To some students, the arts offer sensory experiences as simple as vibrations from music, which give feedback to their bodies and brains as to where they are in space. For other children in the same class, the arts offer different experiences from the same activities: a choice of songs, dance activities and opportunities for self-expression. This awareness of being and the reciprocity of the relationship between teacher and student and between students is founded by the arts-based curriculum.

~~~~~~~~

Drama is integral to the curriculum at PPSS. Children love to pretend and adore the chance to dress up. Indeed, the school has a storeroom filled with so many costumes that you might think you were backstage on Broadway. Bella ensured PPSS had a full-time drama therapist—Amanda Musicka-Williams—and a part-time drama teacher—Dan Dinnen.

Dan once worked with some of the best budding actors in Australia, but after he conducted a workshop with some students from PPSS, he chose to leave the professional stage to devote himself to working with children with intellectual disabilities. Dan teaches his own classes and brainstorms with other PPSS teachers about ways to improve and intensify the drama possibilities in their classrooms. He believes drama is a powerful tool for cognitive development and that it offers an important emotional outlet for children. He also believes the chance to perform is a key opportunity to improve these children's sense of self-worth.

In their own words: All the school's a stage

Dan Dinnen

I ran my first drama workshops in 1996. The students were a diverse bunch of young primary school kids in after-school care. I'd run drama for 90 minutes once a week at a picturesque public school on the southern shores of Sydney Harbour. It was exhausting and I learned a lot! I found out which elements of drama were useful for a group of high energy, easily distracted kids, and which elements didn't work. It was a great opportunity to find out what I had to offer as a drama practitioner and as a facilitator to the dramatic play and interaction of these children.

This process continued in different contexts and with different groups of young people for more than a decade. During that time I worked for the best youth theatre companies in Sydney and Melbourne, and taught some gifted, bright, young people brimming with potential. Occasionally, I'd have a student with that 'X' factor, that ethereal thing called talent, and I came to see that no-one turns another person into an actor. Actors just are. Drama teachers merely provide guidance, structure, feedback, opportunities to explore and a series of scaffolding experiences for growth.

More often than not, the students I worked with were not and never would be professional actors. Yet working with these students I came to see an even greater meaning and reward in the work I was doing. Drama provides something wonderful for every participant. Drama is a safe place to engage in creative communication, to wield your imagination and to know it as valuable and powerful. To engage in drama is to actively and consciously dream—to see beyond the everyday. More than this, drama—

by nature a group exercise—invites us to collaborate in this imaginative world. We play together using human interaction and in doing so we discover truths about ourselves and others. We explore our boundaries and our limitations. And we discover strengths within ourselves.

In 2005, I started teaching some weekly workshops for teenagers with disabilities. The Drama Teens workshops were run by the Joint Councils Access for All Abilities and with few exceptions the students came from PPSS, so they all had intellectual disabilities. I had never worked in special education before this and the experience was a turning point in my life as a teacher. I worked with the Drama Teens students on and off for the next three years. I also became involved with PPSS, first as a casual relief teacher and then in 2007 in a permanent position as a specialist drama teacher.

Starting at PPSS as the newly appointed drama teacher, I was excited and also quite anxious. My proposal to the school was that I would implement a program of drama that focused on *process*, not *product*. My job would not be to produce plays. The school already had a successful program putting on a yearly concert that involved every student. I wanted to engage students in dramatic play itself in the firm belief that this would be good for their communication and living skills, for their cognitive development, for their wellbeing and for their sense of self.

I knew through my experience with Drama Teens that the response from students with intellectual disabilities to pure, process-based drama could be incredibly positive. However, as the drama teacher at PPSS, I faced a timetable of 15 different groups of students of every age and with a much wider range of intellectual disabilities than the groups with which I had previously run drama classes. My instinct that drama would be a good and useful thing for them was to be put to the absolute test. I had to prove it! Several years later the students *are* proving it each and every day that I work with them.

At PPSS I work with many students who have Down syndrome. Many of these students are highly engaged in their drama class activities and readily display the extroverted side to their often large personalities. Individuals with Down syndrome have a higher risk for many conditions that can inhibit their ability to engage easily with others in structured group play. For example, Ethan has poor vision and hearing, as well as limited speech. He can find it difficult to engage directly with his peers and often resorts to pushing others and general rough-housing, because this gives him a satisfying sense of contact with others. Ethan also finds it hard to sit still. He craves attention and distraction, and if he has neither he tends to make loud noises, roll around on the floor and to encroach on others' personal space.

At PPSS I work with the students in a circle, but for the most part we sit rather than stand. I found several activities effective for engaging Ethan fully. One was a simple game that I have introduced with success to many groups at PPSS. The game is called Zap! and it involves passing a loud hand-clap accompanied by the word 'Zap!' around the circle. The actual word can be replaced by any sound or utterance, and for non-verbal students, the physical action can be the primary focus. The Zap! travels from person to person as an exchange of energy. Participants are encouraged to make eye contact with the person they receive the Zap! from, as well as the person they send the Zap! to. Ethan learned this game easily and participated with relish. The loud, physical nature of the exchange was satisfying for him. He was in control of the communicative exchange and, importantly, connected to the whole group during the game, as he could sense the Zap! travelling around the circle.

Another effective way of engaging Ethan was with binoculars. Not real binoculars, but cardboard rolls, stuck together with tape. I was struggling to engage Ethan in greeting games at the start of his drama classes. These games are integral for many of my classes at PPSS. Students are encouraged to greet each other physically, as well as vocally, and this is extended to explore physical expression, voice, imagination and simple emotions in the rest of the class. With the cardboard binoculars, Ethan had a tool to focus his vision on one classmate at a time. He was able to connect with another classmate in a gentle, direct way that did not involve rough physicality. One of my favourite images is of Ethan with the binoculars pressed to his eyes while a classmate looks through the other end. Both are grinning and laughing.

To get students who have autism spectrum disorders engaged in drama has been a challenge. The cardboard binoculars have proven effective with many of these students, as has communicating via puppets and masks. There are certain students, however, whose autism is such an obstacle to engaging in drama that at the end of my first semester as specialist drama teacher at PPSS, I seriously doubted whether I was able to warrant the benefit of drama for these students. People with autism can find it difficult or impossible to recognise and identify emotions in others, to understand abstract expression and the notion of make-believe, and can be highly distressed by environments and situations that are unpredictable and chaotic.

A particular student who was simply not engaging in all of this was Isaac. A junior-school student, Isaac could not seem to settle in the drama room. He was anxious and would run around the room for much of each session. He needed constant reassurance that he would be returning to his regular classroom soon. I really didn't know what to do, other than just forge ahead each week. I ran the class and attempted to involve Isaac with each activity. As weeks passed, Isaac was able to briefly engage in greeting games and in Zap! One activity that I repeated weekly with Isaac's group was asking students to identify the primary emotions using A4-size pictures of happy, sad and angry faces. Students would identify the emotion and then mimic it. We'd then extend this into dramatic play. One day during my second semester with the group, Isaac correctly identified all three faces. He then showed his own happy and sad face, and correctly identified each face when I demonstrated them myself.

My initial response: thank goodness, he's finally participating. However, it was the reaction of the teaching assistant who had known him for some time that made me stop.

'He's never been able to do that!' she said, her face wide-eyed and still with wonder.

This was a huge moment for Isaac and for me. I had learned the lesson of patience. I know now how to read the small signs in my students with autism spectrum disorders, to know that progress is happening slowly, in small ways, and this is potentially leading towards a breakthrough. Isaac had behaviour modelled for him, by me and by others. He witnessed his peers exploring the primary emotions through dramatic play and interaction each week. Although his active participation was sporadic, week by week the rituals of our drama play made more and more sense to Isaac, until he was empowered to join in, to identify happy, sad and angry faces, and to explore his own expression of these emotions for no other purpose than to engage with others in an imaginative way.

***

Jim is a student in the transition school with severe autism and extreme behavioural issues. He is socially withdrawn and prone to violent and destructive outbursts. His behaviour can be highly oppositional and he can be passively and actively aggressive when he doesn't want to do something. At the start of 2008, I had my first drama class with Jim. I knew he responded well to music and he liked to sing, but I had no idea how he would respond to the drama activities I was running in my programs.

Jim responded extremely well to being in a circle and playing greeting games. He enjoyed the attention of having one-on-one engagement with me during these interactions. However, after 10 minutes of focused communicative exchange, Jim would become overexcited and would start to display disruptive or potentially destructive behaviours.

During the first semester, Jim became more attuned to the routine of his weekly drama class and by the second semester he had several sessions where he had significant moments of engagement. Each session for Jim's group began with 10 minutes of relaxation and gentle sensory play. Then the group would sit in a circle and go through a series of greetings and interactions. I had tried to engage the group with puppets as a way to encourage interaction but without much success. During one session I changed tactics and, rather than encouraging the students to use the puppets, I placed several puppets in the centre of the circle. I asked Jim what to name one of the puppets and he immediately supplied a name. We spent the next 10 minutes narrating a series of interactions and simple sequences for the puppets to enact. I would suggest something, for example, 'Should the puppets wake up?', and Jim would reply, 'Yes!'

'Should they yawn?'

'Yes, yawn!'

'What should they do next?'

'Say hello!'

This was significant. While Jim had not interacted with me or his classmates in such rudimentary play before, now he was totally engaged, focused and enjoying himself. During another session, I successfully engaged Jim in imaginative play using a different technique. I demonstrated how to use your first two fingers as a little 'person' that can walk across the floor, up your arm, and so on. Jim was taken with this and little Dan and little Jim walked around, lay down, woke up, said hello, went climbing mountains and generally had a wonderful time.

On both occasions, Jim was able to engage in these activities without getting overexcited and he was able to complete the session without having to have time-out—an outcome that had been the exception rather than the rule. During our classes together, I became aware that sustained eye contact tends to be a trigger for Jim to become overstimulated. The same goes for using heightened vocal inflections too much. Interactions with Jim can be sustained for longer periods with positive effect by carefully winding back the energy in my voice and using my eye contact sparingly. By placing the focus of an interaction onto puppets, Jim is able to explore dramatic play at a remove from himself. The use of our fingers as little people has the same effect and Jim can play, interact and engage in an imaginative communicative realm without it overwhelming him.

I've now been working at PPSS as a drama specialist for several years. Working with students with a range of intellectual disabilities across all age groups has led me to question and to redefine: What *is* drama? What can it be and what should it be in the context of this school and these students? I had defined drama as active, conscious dreaming, as seeing beyond the everyday, as collaboration in the imaginative world. There are students at PPSS who are not able to verbalise and who cannot demonstrate meta-cognitive skills—that is, they can't demonstrate an awareness of their own thinking and learning processes—so it can't easily be shown that these students are consciously and collaboratively wielding their imaginations.

Part of my work has shifted, from an understanding of drama as being by nature a group exercise, to an emphasis on one-on-one interactions within the context of group work, as with Jim's sessions. And the emphasis with many students is simply to engage them in play. To play, to make sounds and gestures for no other reason than pure exploration, expression and fun is something that we can too easily take for granted. Yet these skills are fundamental to cognitive development. To play with a toy. To imagine that it is animate, that it has a life, that it can be manipulated. That an object can be something other than itself. And that a person can be something else, someone else, somewhere else ...

Drama is playing make-believe, dressing up, telling and re-enacting stories, putting on puppet shows and engaging in narratives. Drama is greeting each other with silly voices, pretending to be someone else, exploring our range of movement and gesture, singing songs and playing games. But if there is an absolute essence, drama is pure communicative exchange for the sake of it. The outcome may be as simple as a moment of sustained eye contact, a smile, laugh or moment of reaction. This essence may be enough. And it is often the beginning of much more.

Chapter 7
How art changes the brain

···

Any parent or educator knows intuitively the power of the arts. Who hasn't taught their child to learn the alphabet by singing that familiar song? Taught simple counting through rhymes like, 'One, Two, Buckle My Shoe'? Or wondered where on earth their three-year-old picked up a swear word, and then realised it came from listening to the radio on the drive to kindergarten!

Yet using the arts to their full potential in a classroom setting is something that has often eluded educators. Do the arts seem too much like fun? Should school be more like work? Bella Irlicht's decision to implement a Visual and Performing Arts Curriculum at Port Phillip Specialist School was born of her observations that whenever children were singing, dancing, painting or play-acting, they seemed more engaged and happy.

The curriculum change was carefully considered and implemented. The teachers at PPSS had documented what their students seemed to enjoy most and seemed to learn. There was evidence that many students at PPSS attended outside activities that involved the arts. There were also numerous instances in the literature in which people with disabilities seemed to benefit from arts-based therapies (Pring et al. 1997; Sacks 2007).

The research evidence that Carl Parsons has started to collect shows that the arts can change the brain and assist in learning, and should be considered an important tool for teaching and learning. Research is validating the experiences of those at PPSS: the arts can change and improve learning.

~~~~~~~~~~

Art and neuroscience

Carl Parsons

Over the years, there has been an increasing emphasis on understanding the importance of the arts for learning (Burton et al. 1999; Darby

& Catterall 1994; Deasy 2002; Fogg & Smith 2001; Gullatt 2008; Hamblen 1993; Heath & Roach 1999; Mason et al. 2004; Winner & Hetland 2000; Zimmerman 1997). Much of this work has shown that students who participate in arts activities on a regular basis have higher achievement levels than students who do not participate in arts activities (Eisner 1998). Results have also shown that students who participate in arts-based activities do better in core subjects (including reading, writing, maths, science and language) than students who do not participate in arts-based activities (McMahon et al. 2003). Students who participate in arts-based activities have a higher emotional intelligence and lower dropout rates from school. (For a fuller review, please see Sandra S. Ruppert's 2006 work, *Critical Evidence: How the Arts Benefit Student Achievement.*)

As these achievements have been studied, there has been an increase in understanding of the role of arts in cognitive development (Blakemore & Frith 2005; Byrnes 2001; Dana Foundation 2005; Dunbar 2008; Elfand 2002; Ellis 1999; Posner et al. 2008; Spelke 2008). The majority of this research has shown that arts help develop the cognitive abilities of the brain (Gardiner et al. 1996). Thus, neurosciences and visual and performing arts are intertwined (Berg 2010; Brown & Parsons 2008; Rose 2004).

Indeed, there is evidence that visual and performing arts activities causes changes in the brain (Berrol 2006; Blood et al. 1999; Carlsson et al. 2000; Chen et al. 2008; Davis & Thaut 1989; Kowatari et al. 2009).

Science has shown that the brain is dynamic and not fixed as once thought (Doidge 2007; Greenough et al. 1987; Jensen 2001). We know that the brain is growing new neurons, making new connections, allowing neurons and connections not being used to die, and changing its own chemistry constantly—thus reorganising itself (Grezes et al. 1999; Moreno et al. 2009; Zaidel 2010).

It has been shown that educational activities can change the brain. Yes, that means teaching, and teachers, can change a brain (Alward et al. 2003; Draganski et al. 2004; Greenough et al. 1987; Grezes et al. 1999).

Teaching can also influence stress levels. People don't learn as well when they are stressed (McEwen 2000a, 2000b, 2000c). People learn best during activities they enjoy, and they are likely to spend more time doing activities they enjoy. Using enjoyable activities is more likely to get positive results in building new skills and gives us an opportunity to incorporate new learning into these activities.

There are numerous reports of people with disabilities who had a propensity to learn through the visual and performing arts (Damasio 1994; Wallace et al. 2009).

There is also ample evidence that students with disabilities benefit from learning activities that employ visual and performing arts (Brown 1994; Brownwell 2002; Buday 1995; Essex et al. 1996; Jellison et al. 1984; Katagiri 2009; Pasiali 2004; Torrance 2003; Wheeler & Carter 1998).

At PPSS, we have attempted to use the arts to extend each student's individual learning abilities. That is, extend their learning into areas they are ready to move in to. We have also worked hard to embed traditional aspects of the curriculum (listening, following instructions, communication, reading, writing, spelling, daily living skills, numeracy and social skills) into the arts.

An evolving model

PPSS has attempted to discover the interests and skills of students, reviewed the research on the effect of visual and performing arts that showed positive outcomes and has implemented a new curriculum. The Visual and Performing Arts Curriculum is an attempt to extend the skills of students through the visual and performing arts.

As we have mentioned in the previous chapter, it is important to recognise that we are not teaching students to become visual and performing artists. We use the visual and performing arts to motivate students and teach the curriculum. However, the goals set are around communication and literacy, numeracy, daily living and social skills. The arts are a way to teach these goals.

All goals are worked on in classroom activities. When possible, teachers use various aspects of the visual and performing arts activities identified above. Students also attend specialist classes where they focus on visual and performing arts activities, but their goals are always the same and are worked on in these sessions.

For example, a team of staff and family members may decide that a particular student needs to learn to listen carefully to instructions. This goal is worked on in the classroom in art, dance, drama, music, swimming and physical education classes.

The model for embedding all goals is still evolving. Increasingly, teachers, teacher assistants, therapists and specialist teachers are finding new ways to use visual and performing arts to help students achieve their goals. There is no map that tells us how to do this. The school has trialled numerous strategies including: teachers identifying ways to teach using visual and performing arts; specialists working in the classroom; specialists visiting classrooms and giving teachers advice on visual and performing arts strategies that may help to achieve a particular goal; and having art, drama and music therapists work one-on-one with children when appropriate. While all of this input has been positive and staff have become skilled, there is still more to learn and more to trial. The only way we will achieve our goal is when our students achieve the goals we have set for them.

All staff members are committed to using a VPAC. The school has become a leader in using the Visual and Performing Arts Curriculum. Our students are motivated and happy. Only time and systematic research will tell us if this is best practice for educating students with disabilities. We are working on strategies to help evaluate the effectiveness of the VPAC (Riccio et al. 2003).

~~~~~~~~~~

How did PPSS find such talented and diverse arts educators to teach at the school? Bella says a principal needs to be a talent scout. The school's first dance teacher was Jeanette Liddell, who was one of Australia's leading contemporary dancers. Jeanette had volunteered at the school, and her classes were so successful that when she gave up teaching, Bella knew the school needed a full-time replacement. First, Bella looked in-house. Teaching assistant Cathy Rendall had a background in dance and Bella encouraged her to expand her role at the school. Bella remembers that Cathy was quite shy, but quickly gained confidence as she realised how much she could teach the children. By the time of the RiSE Symposium in 2008, Cathy had the poise to present her findings to an audience of hundreds.

~~~~~~~~~~

In practice: Dancing our way to learning

'Okay, let's listen everybody!' dance teacher Cathy Rendall calls out, clapping her hands. 'How many students are here today?'

After pointing to each student in turn, a tall boy answers, 'Seventeen!'

'That's right. Now take away three for the Victorian College of Arts students who are visiting us today, Eric. How many are left?'

A pause. 'Fourteen,' Eric responds.

'Good work! Fourteen. We need to divide into two groups. Who knows how many that makes in each group?'

A hand shoots up. 'Seven!'

'Right, Audrey. Two groups of seven. Now half of you are the audience and half are dancing, then we switch. Ready?' Cathy flicks a switch on the music player and the sound of 'Poker Face' pulsates through the studio. Hips gyrate and hands sway, as Cathy leads the class through an energetic modern dance routine of the sort you might expect to see in a posh studio. The impression is punctured by a calm voice over the loudspeaker.

'Code Green, Code Green.' Nicki, a teaching assistant, leaps to her feet and darts for the door. The announcement means a student is unaccounted for. It's the job of all assistant teachers to stop whatever they are doing to find the student. The various playgrounds and courtyards at the school offer students as much autonomy as possible, but there are also safeguards—like Code Green—to make sure emerging independence doesn't lead to grief. In less than a minute, Nicki is back—mission accomplished.

In the meantime, Cathy and her class haven't missed a beat and are learning a new move courtesy of one of the students.

'Step, slide, step, slide—great idea, Tyrell,' Cathy smiles, immediately incorporating the boy's improvisation into the routine as Tyrell beams.

In Cathy's class, as elsewhere at PPSS, communication, numeracy and living skills are all incorporated into art in a way that is seamless and organic. It is also highly individualised.

After class, Cathy turns on her computer and shows a flowchart—part of a computer program that she uses for all of her classes. The program documents the particular dance routines and lessons she teaches, as well as keeping track of student goals, skills being taught and how each child is faring. After each class, she types in a quick note about each student's performance that day. Over time, these notes demonstrate trends, which in turn help her assess how to improve her lessons. Cathy's dance class is a separate session, but she is also working in collaboration with classroom teachers and other therapists to target each of the children's student support group goals.

Such computer post-class analysis is required of every teacher, therapist and specialist in every class and session at the school. Over time, the collective trends and patterns captured by this data reveal a broader and more nuanced portrait of how each individual child is faring. Together, teachers, therapists, specialists and senior staff are then able to assess and alter each child's program, after seeing what is working and what is not.

This crucial reporting and assessment tool is a variation of one initially developed exclusively for the Lutheran schools by Melbourne-based education consultant Pam Russell. After obtaining permission from the Lutheran education association, Pam offered to adapt the program pro bono so that it could be used at PPSS.

As an example, this program helped Cathy spot that one young boy consistently struggled to focus. Dance involves movement in space and a dance studio is a large, open space with abstract concepts; for example, front, back, left, right, and so on. The classroom was too stimulating and he seemed not to know where he should be in the space.

'I taped an "X" on the floor on his spot. That helped. Then, I had an even better idea,' Cathy explains.

Cathy goes to the prop room and returns with a large paper flower, a metre high. Its stalk is a cardboard cylinder, with construction paper leaves and petals. 'I put this flower on the X.'

The student could visualise his spot in the room, which helped him to focus, to participate with the group and calm his emotions. This young boy was visually impaired and had spatial problems, and he was now able to engage with this activity with great enthusiasm. It was a 'magic moment'.

Such magic moments are what keep all teachers going. A girl with autism in one of Cathy's classes, who'd spent months facing the wall as her classmates went through their dance moves, showed a glimmer of interest in a new routine.

'We were doing a cheerleading dance and I offered her a choice between two pairs of pompoms,' Cathy remembers. 'She chose blue. Then, to my amazement, she stood up and started to dance, still facing the back of the room. We don't have mirrors here, because they distract our students. Yet somehow she'd memorised every single step. It was perfect. I had goose bumps.'

Recognising how props could be powerful tools to help children learn gave Cathy another idea. Staff collaboration is a hallmark of PPSS and recently Cathy began working with art therapist Anita Bragge to create life-sized dancing puppets. Anita created the stuffed puppets with some of her students and then together they toyed with different ways to anchor the puppets to their hands and feet. The idea is that when a student dances, the puppet performs the identical moves in front of them.

'Somehow, it makes it easier for students to focus on a sequence of dance steps, because you are making the puppet move and they have a visual tool to work with. Through movement the students were able to connect with the puppet, promoting individuality and creativity,' Cathy explains.

Not all experiments work, of course. To encourage innovation during her time as principal, Bella Irlicht strove to create an artistic culture that applauded and implemented successful ideas and jettisoned failures without chastising the teacher, therapist or specialist staff member. That culture continues under principal Robert Newall, which explains why the school is constantly evolving.

For Cathy, teaching dance at PPSS is a natural extension of who she is.

'I was one of three sisters,' she explains, 'and I remember as a child travelling in the car and seeing a bus with special children and thinking, "I'm glad that's not me or my sisters." Then Mum got pregnant and we were all excited. We couldn't wait to see the baby. But it took forever for Mum to come home from the hospital. When she did, she sat us all down on the bed and told us our new little sister had Down syndrome. And I said, "Not like those kids on the bus!" And then we all cried.'

Cathy pauses. 'I can't believe I said that. But pretty soon we were fighting to see who could take care of Ali. When I used to practise dancing, Ali wanted to dance with me and I loved teaching her. She would mimic everything I did and would always want to do more. We sisters performed for our parents every week, showing off our new moves.'

Cathy points to a picture of a charming little girl with perfect pigtails, wearing a tutu and a dazzling smile. 'Ali's my inspiration,' she says simply.

Cathy turns off the computer to prepare for her next class. These are the little children and Cathy has laid out a collection of hula hoops, as well as various different-shaped mats.

'It's so easy to teach shapes through dance. We also make patterns in the dances themselves—circles, squares, lines and so on.' Cathy explains how concepts are taught through the words of familiar songs—like 'Five Little Ducks' and 'The Wheels on the Bus'—as well as through incorporating props. Sit *on* the seat. Get *under* the umbrella. Stand *behind* the yellow duck: abstract concepts that make a lot more sense in context.

While the life-sized dancing puppets are a recent experiment, everyone at PPSS knows the power of costumes as a learning tool to teach children to dress themselves. Over the head, here's the zip, a button or two—it's all good fun.

Cathy slides her hand across a clothes rack full of costume choices. 'Lollipops, from when we did a scene from the *Wizard of Oz* for the international symposium we hosted in 2008. The kids loved that routine.' Her fingers fly through the collection of fairy wings, princess gowns, superhero capes, as well as lions, tigers and tulle.

The next class of children troop in. They have bright eyes and gleeful expressions.

'Sit on the mat!' one boy chortles exuberantly, as Cathy tells the kids to do just that, her words always accompanied by the gestures of key word signing. The children sit in a wiggly, raggedy circle. Cathy points to a Time Timer sitting next to her on the floor. It is set for 30 minutes, and this shows as a red wedge. As the dial turns, the red disappears. When the timer dings, there is no red left and the students have a visible, as well as audible, reminder that class has finished. It's a big support for those who struggle with transitioning from one activity to the next.

Like other teachers here, Cathy knows other tips for helping children break down a complicated concept like time. To use a sports metaphor, she telegraphs the play. Cathy claps her hands for attention. 'Look at me,' she says, gesturing to her eyes. 'First, we sit on the mat. Then we warm up. Then costumes. And after dance class is finished, you go back to class for morning tea. Now, let's get started.'

Any dance class for four-year-old children is not totally structured. There is a lot of jumping up and down, and exuberant shimmying. But what feels free and easy to the children actually has a complex hidden structure because the beauty of the dance masks the choreography beneath. It is a choreography that not only lies at the heart of this class, but at the heart of PPSS. Every element of the curriculum is planned, orchestrated and broken down into small pieces. There's plenty of room for improvisation from students or teachers. But the goal is a complex routine comprised of myriad tiny, discrete steps. Performed on its own, each step is simple enough. Over time and with practice, the steps are linked together until complex patterns emerge and the children's skills extend and deepen.

As the timer dings, it appears class is over. But not really. Because each class is woven to the one before and the one after in another kind of choreography.

~~~~~~~~~

Two paintings hang on opposite walls in the central corridor of PPSS. Both are bold, abstract and arresting—one in fiery oranges, the other in aquatic greens and blues. But their position on the walls isn't the only factor that divides them.

'Can you tell the difference?' asks principal Rob Newall asks with a wry smile. Clearly this is a trick question. 'One is art,' Rob points to the green painting. 'The other is not.'

As I appeared perplexed, he reveals, 'It isn't art, but art therapy. It's the by-product of a therapy session, which happens to be expressed through a visual medium. And that's different from art, which is a conscious, creative, visual expression. While you can't tell the difference with the naked eye, there's even a debate about whether therapy canvases should be hung at all.'

That both these works are on display is evidence of the importance PPSS places on both disciplines. PPSS is accustomed to using media in a variety of ways. Even art class isn't quite what you might expect at a traditional school. Here, students are working on broader goals than simply creating an attractive picture or sculpture. Communication, fine motor and living skills are just some of the abilities that are fostered during an art class with teacher Ross Denby. Ross' cheerful demeanour gives no hint that his understanding of the students is as personal as it is profound.

~~~~~~~~~

In practice: How the world looks to me
- -

The art room at PPSS is a large, charmingly messy and paint-splattered room. A zebra print covers much of one wall. A print of Vincent Van Gogh's self-portrait is on the back of the door and a print of Claude Monet's impressionist study of water lilies graces another wall. In the centre of a long, rectangular table is a bowl of green pears: a still life.

'How many pears are there? Who can count them?' art teacher Ross Denby asks. 'Yes, that's right, there are three,' he nods. There's no escape from numeracy at PPSS, even in art class.

Ross is holding what looks like a window frame, and the children—wearing art smocks over their navy and gold uniforms—are pressed against the table, intrigued.

'Today we are not going to draw, but we will paint in a different way,' Ross explains. He lifts the wooden screen printing frame up to his face as the children gape. 'See, this is like a window. I can look through it, and I can see you and you can see me. But in the fabric in this window I have cut three shapes ... what are they? You're right, they're pears. We're going to run paint over this fabric and the stencil will force paint onto the open areas printing the design of our pears. Who goes first?'

Every hand is raised high and wiggling exuberantly. As Ross selects the first boy to use the stencil, other children jostle to use the squeegee—the rubber tool perfect for manipulating gooey paint across the screen. Is this occupational therapy? A test of fine motor skills? No, it's art—a creative outlet that results in a cool picture. The extra learning that is immediately apparent to an observer is invisible to the children.

'Who can tell me how to make the colour green?' Ross asks, offering an impromptu lesson in primary and secondary colours as he works with one child. 'Now look, the paint went through the holes and squeezed onto the paper and look what we have—three pears!' The kids ooh and ahh, and one child claps. 'It's called silk screening,' Ross explains. 'It's a kind of traditional printing. And because we're printing, we can make a copy for each of you.'

As one boy labours over the frame and tools, teacher's aide Helen Doyle signs and sings the entire lesson for another boy, so he can better understand what he hears. 'Kyle is printing, printing, printing. Kyle is printing, printing three pears.'

Meanwhile, Ross pulls out a magnifying glass and allows another boy to examine the pears. 'What do you notice about their skin?' Ross asks.

'Oh!' the boy exclaims, 'there are lots of little dots!'

'Exactly! But now look. You don't see them from a distance. They disappear. Why?' Ross explains perspective, then pops another question. 'And what about this? What's this little piece at the top of the pear?'

'A stem!' a girl answers.

'Exactly! We're going to make stems on our pictures out of leather. Look, I have this book of leather samples and we can choose the colour that matches each pear best. But why does a pear have a stem anyway? What is it for?'

From using a magnifying glass to mixing paint, from the study of living things to understanding the complexities of perspective, from the mechanics of a graphic design to the intricacies of the colour wheel, art for art's sake is only the beginning at PPSS. Art means science, maths, communication and self-expression.

Art isn't just beautiful, art is elemental and essential. The act of creating art is a fundamental human impulse and it is a powerful tool for teaching all children, especially children for whom learning is, and always will be, more difficult.

Ross works with students not only in art class, but in the school's end-of-year concerts, which he has produced for several years. He has taught at PPSS for a decade, but his knowledge of children with disabilities goes back further than that.

Later, Ross elaborates. 'Our second child was a boy. We named him Paul. He had an intellectual disability and adrenoleukodystrophy ... the same disease portrayed in the movie *Lorenzo's Oil*. I had been teaching in a secondary college, but ultimately left to stay home with our son. He was 14 years old when he died, in 1999.

'A few months after Paul's death, the principal of his specialist school called and told me, "I think it's time you got back to work." I decided to take an art job at a special school and discovered I really liked it. Then I learned about the position here. Bella would back any halfway reasonable idea, and the school was full of possibilities—very vibrant,' Ross says.

'I don't look at these children as if they are broken. I don't well up with tears and think, "Oh, you poor thing." I take them as they are, and I try to bring out what I can through the arts. I try to be dispassionate.'

Ross pauses as a memory interrupts. 'There was one time, though. One time in the 10 years I've been here,' he amends.

Ross had been helping out in the swimming program one day, helping a student in the change room to put on his bathers. He looked down and saw that the boy had a percutaneous endoscopic gastrostomy tube (PEG), to allow the child to be given food or medicine directly into his body.

'And it reminded me of Paul,' Ross says. 'Then the weirdest thing happened, totally out of the blue. I looked down at the top of his little head and just like that I broke down. I called out, "I can't do this!" and handed him over and ran out of that room.'

There is another lengthy pause as Ross composes himself.

'I thought, where did that come from? All those years later? But you never really get over the trauma of losing a child. You think you have, you've gone through the process and you have, but always there is that little hole.'

Like Ross, many of the staff at PPSS have a personal relationship with disability. It gives them greater understanding of the many ways in which having a child with a disability affects a family, but it can also be overwhelming on occasion.

Ros Jennings, the PPSS social worker, explains. 'It's crucial for us to be here for the staff, as well as to provide support for families and students,' Ros says. 'That's especially true when it comes to our students whose disability has a terminal prognosis. These children have very little time on earth and the time they have is precious. We want to make it special, in every way that we can. But we also know that caring for our students can be emotionally wrenching for our staff. The illness or death of a student can dredge up their own loss and sorrow. It's part of working in a special school.'

Principal Rob Newall explains. 'In any special school, the average length of time that a teacher stays is three years. Just three years! Many of our staff have stayed much longer than that. Partly, that's because this is a creative, exciting school. But we also think part of good staff retention is that we try to support our teachers, therapists and specialists. We try to give them new chances to learn outside school, as well as rotating assignments here in school. We also have informal get-togethers. We know they need our support. We also know that working in a special school is highly rewarding, and provides a lot of joy, ' Rob says.

Ross agrees. 'I love being with these students. One of my favourite things about working in a specialist school is that I don't have any expectations of what is going to come out of an art class. I throw things up in the air, and they land differently every time—it's impossible to predict,' he says.

'If I have a class of children who are primarily on the autism spectrum and need routine, it doesn't mean I have to use the same medium every time. I might create routine through structured greetings, roll call and the like,' Ross explains.

'I'm always looking for new ideas. I think next term I might try some new settling activities, like getting children to put their hands in a bowl of water to relax before we start,' he says.

The non-verbal nature of art is a boon to students with limited speech, and sometimes putting paint to paper can be like finding the source of an underground spring as a child discovers a new way to tap into his inner world. Ross remembers a student who laboured over one painting, a swirling mass of browns and reds. The painting was arresting, but Ross wasn't sure what it represented. When he asked, the boy replied simply, 'Tsunami.'

'Art is a vital means of expression. It's transcendent and universal,' Ross says. 'There is always something you can find they respond to. Maybe they don't like painting, but they like clay, papier-mâché or print making. I always try new things.

'You know when astronomers discover a new star or something in the galaxy? They don't know anything much about it: its atmosphere or environment. Everything is foreign. A mystery. Unexplored.

'I often think of our children that way: as new worlds, completely unknown and uncharted. We can't look at them like our world—they won't ever be exactly like us. You have to set aside preconceptions and be prepared to explore, because each child here is unique,' he says.

The screen-printing lesson has been a big hit. One girl looks up at Ross. 'Can I sign mine?' she asks proudly, as she uses a hair dryer to blow-dry her print.

'Certainly! You can write in block letters, or any way you choose,' Ross responds.

The girl looks up, and her smile is dazzling.

~~~~~~

It is not difficult to get Bella to rave about the extraordinary teaching faculty at PPSS, including middle-school teacher Bronwyn Welch. Bella noted:

> *Bronwyn was a music therapist before she became a special education teacher. She plays double bass in various orchestras and uses a guitar in class. Bronwyn*

never raises her voice, but always uses music to teach and control the children. I used to sit in on her classes for inspiration. I remember one day she was working with a class of students with severe autism. She was teaching them how to read by making a cake! First, Bronwyn broke the task into small jobs that she wrote on the board as sentences beginning with a different child's name. Then she put those sentences to music and sang the song as she used her finger to track the words. Soon the students could read the entire song! This is what we mean by using the arts to teach.

~~~~~~~~~

In their own words: Sing me to read

Bronwyn Welch

I'm sure some people might find it challenging to work at a school where you need to use the arts, no matter what subject you teach. But I can't imagine teaching any other way.

I've taught in the junior and middle schools. In both environments, I find that what works best is to use the arts in combination with other programs. That's how I'm best able to help our students with a wide range of literacy and numeracy skills.

Communicating and counting

At PPSS, while all the children have an intellectual disability, there is a wide range of skills and abilities. Several of the students in my class are quite social in that they enjoy watching the other students in the class, but find it difficult to initiate and sustain an interaction with their peers.

Music often comes to the rescue. As part of our morning circle routine, we sing 'Six Grey Elephants Balancing'. This song has several objectives: to encourage the students to interact with each other on verbal and non-verbal levels, and to develop counting skills.

I can't think of that song without remembering a wonderful boy named Dennis. He particularly enjoyed participating in this song and would often choose the Picture Communication Symbol of an elephant from the board to make his choice crystal clear. Then he would hold his arm out as if it were a trunk to show that he was an elephant and parade around the room. Humour is enticing for children and Dennis loved pretending to be an elephant balancing on a piece of string so much. He never thought of it as a chance to work on his coordination, balance and concentration!

But even more motivating for Dennis was that as the song continued, he was asked to choose the next student to parade around the room with him. This he did enthusiastically, approaching other students at the end of each verse. One by one, Dennis's friends joined the line of elephants and joined in the song. While talking is difficult for Dennis, he was so keen to have his friends join in that he would point to each person by turn, beckon with his hand and attempt to say the word 'come'. Lining his friends up against the wall in his train of elephants, he then proceeded to count them. Dennis would point to each child by turn, saying 'un, oo, eee' (one, two, three) before laughing and giving himself a round of applause. Dennis had just given himself a speech therapy class, as well as a numeracy session. But from the outside, it might have appeared he was 'just playing'.

Using drama when words fail

Drama is something we teach, but drama is also an innate trait in many children. As they become comfortable with play-acting, as they see that we take it seriously and even incorporate it into the class, it becomes a tool for them as well as for us. One day a girl named Elyse gave me a great example of that. Elyse always enjoyed listening to stories and looking at the pictures in books; however, she didn't have the communication skills to articulate what happened next. That's an important skill because it indicates what children remember, as well as giving children a sense of order and predictability. Each time the story is read, it turns out the same way. Routine and order are soothing for children.

One day, while reading a favourite big book, I stopped reading halfway through and before turning the page asked, as I always did, 'What happened next?' That day, Elyse slid off her chair onto the floor, lay down and pretended to go to sleep. 'That's right, Elyse!' I said. 'The animals all went to sleep.'

Using songs to understand positions

Language is filled with all sorts of words that are really quite complicated concepts. Prepositions are a great example. Words like 'over', 'under', 'between' and 'with' aren't objects, like a dog or a sock. They aren't actions that we can demonstrate, like running or jumping.

And yet they are important. Teachers and parents often use instructions that are filled with prepositions. Hang your bag 'on the hook', walk 'over there', put the toy car 'between the chairs', and so on. In order to teach our students how to listen to an instruction that includes a preposition—such as 'under the table'—we often try using a song to make the task more enjoyable.

Using a familiar tune, we replace the words using favourite toys to teach concepts such as on, under, next to and behind. This takes a lot of concentration, not only for the students but for staff as well, as the lyrics are improvised on the spot! Of course, that's also what makes it so much fun. The end result might be something like:

> Oh, Mia put the teddy under Simon's chair,
> Mia put the teddy under Simon's chair,
> Mia put the teddy under Simon's chair,
> And we all shout 'Hooray!'

Although this is a challenge for both staff and students, it is fun to watch the students listen carefully and then attempt to follow the song. Watching some of the more capable students sneakily trying to help their classmates by pointing and gesturing is quite amusing—and they think I don't notice!

Creating a procedural text

One of our themes for one term centred on the idea of growing. As part of this, we planted some seeds in pots and watched them grow and develop over several weeks. We all had a great deal of fun putting the dirt into the pots and planting the seeds, but many of the students had difficulty in recalling what we did in the planting process.

Using the tune of a familiar song, we rewrote the words of the song, describing the process of planting the seeds. The resulting song was:

> Evan put the dirt in the pot.
> And Brittany put the seeds in the dirt.
> Rose gave the seeds a drink of water.
> And Mark put the seeds in the sun.
> We waited and waited for the seeds to sprout.
> It took about 10 days.
> Colin and Peter were very excited.
> Violet put the plants in the junior yard.

The song was written out on a large piece of paper and displayed in the classroom with photos of the students planting and tending to the seeds. The combination of the music, as well as seeing images of themselves doing the actions, helped to cement the concepts we were teaching. This became one of our favourite songs, and was sung at various times throughout the week.

Singing and drawing—is this work?

Evan had limited verbal skills due to a speech difficulty. He was also extremely strong willed and displayed a number of challenging behaviours. As part of the morning circle routine, the class had been learning the alphabet song 'Ants in the Apple'. Despite his perfect-pitch singing voice, Evan was often reluctant to join in as he couldn't pronounce the words properly and would make approximations of the words. One day in literacy, I drew a picture of a zebra and started singing the verse that corresponded to the letter Z from the song. By combining one art with another and by giving Evan an opportunity to perform on his own, as opposed to being part of the group, Evan was able to complete the task. We completed several other drawings based on the song and I videoed him drawing and singing. Over 10 years at PPSS, Evan continued to make progress. He now communicates, he is learning to read and his behaviour has improved dramatically. His mother, Anita Darlow, says simply, 'He is a different child.'

Learning sight words using music, art and drama

All of the eight students in one class were learning sight words from a standard list of such words known as the *Magic 100 Words* (Reiter 2002, 2003). But for various reasons, all of the students were learning different words. This presented a problem for teaching the students as a group—how could the students learn their individual sight words together in a manner that incorporated the visual and performing arts? All of the students were at such different levels in their learning of words and several of the students were highly competitive, which made creating the program quite a challenge.

After a lot of thought, I developed a literacy program that was based on the visual and performing arts and reflected the varying needs and abilities of the students in the class. Each literacy session (there were three sessions a week) followed a set sequence of activities. We started with the individual lists of 10 sight words that reflected a student's level of learning. Each student came out to the front of the class and sang his or her list of sight words while pointing to each word in turn. The words were stuck with double-sided tape on a board and the order of the words could be changed to prevent students from memorising their list of words. One or two new words were added to the list and old words were taken away as the students became competent in their words.

Following this, we read a story together from a big book and then acted out the story. This was a great source of amusement as the students became different characters and attempted to understand what was really happening in the story. I then asked each student to look at the words on one of the pages of the story and find one of their individual sight words in the text. We would then draw pictures and write sentences that were inspired from the story.

Once the class was familiar with the literacy routine, it seemed less like work and more like having fun. In a 40-minute session, the only part that felt like work to many of the students was the writing activity at the end of the session. The most exciting part of this program was watching the students learn to recognise more and more sight words, and watching their enthusiasm grow as they saw new words being added to their list of sight words. One particular student, who became easily discouraged by his difficulty with reading, was often seen singing the words in his spare time. What really touched me was that he sang not only his own list, but the other children's too.

VPAC literacy and challenging behaviour

In 2005 and 2006, the junior school ran a whole-school literacy program where all students were placed in literacy groups outside of their regular classrooms depending upon their individual literacy needs. One group was for students who were reading, another for students who were beginning to understand sight words and letters, a third group for students who were working on structured table-top activities and a fourth group that did sensory activities. While these groups had the potential to work well, there were four students in these groups with challenging behaviours that were not coping in the program.

After much discussion, it was decided that we would form a separate group specifically for these four students. Art therapist Anita Bragge and I ran this group. In the structured program, we ran the same format each session, but the activities were highly individualised. We began each session with several songs using Picture Exchange Communication System (PECS) pictures to represent the songs. A big book story followed this, and then we would work at the table in one-on-one art activities developing pictures or craft items (such as masks) together with words that reflected the story.

Initially, this was a volatile part of the week, full of protests of varying degrees, but within a term we were starting to see progress. By the end of the year, this program was one of the highlights of the week. Everyone understood the routine and we were producing great works of art that were displayed in classrooms and around the junior hall.

When I first began teaching at PPSS, I found it a huge challenge to use my background in music and my limited knowledge of drama and visual arts to teach literacy, numeracy and social skills. Working together with other teachers, specialists and therapists helped me to explore the possibilities of using the visual and performing arts as the main tool in my teaching. Now I don't think I could do it any other way.

Chapter 8
Proof of performance

· ·

What is it that makes PPSS so special? It is the weaving together of three crucial components: the fact that this is a fully-serviced school, in which the staff members are talented and dedicated; the school's integrated approach, powered by the Integrated Services Committee; and the school's commitment to its innovative Visual and Performing Arts Curriculum.

But there is something else, something a little harder to define. It's the way the school *feels*. It's a vibrant, happy place, where it seems that you just might be able to achieve anything. The people who work here, the parents who bring their children here and, most importantly, the students themselves seem to recognise that they are part of something special. While Bella Irlicht has retired, the proof of performance is that the school endures and the dream of quality special education lives on.

A story illustrates the point. One day, as I was interviewing PPSS principal Robert Newall, he looked a bit distracted. Rob was intermittently staring out of his office window to track the movements of a teenage student playing basketball in the school grounds.

When I asked why he was so interested in this particular boy, Rob answered, 'Dennis is one of the most challenging students we have. He takes up a lot of resources, a lot of time and attention from his teacher, the therapy team, all of us. Recently, Dennis's misbehaviour caused him to be removed from the school bus. Since there really isn't anyone to drive him, and he lives pretty far away, that effectively meant no school.'

I look outside. Clearly the boy is still attending.

'Did you make an exception?'

Rob shakes his head. 'The only reason Dennis is at school is that he *runs five kilometres to get here!*' Rob pauses. 'The running potentially allows him to access a calmer place from where he is *more likely* to pay attention.

Dennis could stop attending school; instead, he chooses to come to school, as he knows we will always look after him and provide secure boundaries.'

Vice-principal Alison Druce is engaged in a lively conversation with a happy, engaging girl. As the girl departs, I ask Alison what she believes sets PPSS apart, since she has worked at other specialist schools in Victoria and New South Wales.

'You know that little girl?' Alison asks. She holds out her hand, which bears a small, distinct scar. 'That's from five years ago, when she bit me. My husband wanted to know why I stayed in special education,' Alison reflects.

'But as we worked with her, we discovered that at the heart of her violent outbursts was tremendous grief that she was physically unable to articulate when a favourite teacher had left the school. We spent months working with her on coping with transitions and we still do. You see the results,' she beams. 'I love having her come to my office!'

After first working for PPSS, Alison had to change her job several times when her husband needed to move for work. She says after working at PPSS, returning to a more traditional special education environment was hard work.

'I was spoiled from working at PPSS. I'm a big believer in what we do here,' Alison says. 'I remember working in one school in which the children had tremendous physical as well as intellectual disabilities. And yet we were following the state curriculum, which included trying to teach them things like the life cycle of frogs. To me, it made no sense! These children found it incredibly difficult to learn and there were a lot more important skills for them to master than understanding about tadpoles.'

Alison says she adapted her lessons at these schools using skills she'd honed at PPSS, but couldn't wait to return to PPSS. When asked what she believes is the number one advantage the school offers, Alison refers to a different sort of life cycle.

'I think it all comes down to how we raise these students. When I look at the young men and women in our transition program, who are about to graduate, I think about how far they and their families have come from when they first entered those gates.

'I have never, at any school where I have worked, seen young men and women who are better educated in the things that matter most. Who are happier, better adjusted, better integrated into their families, with a stronger sense of who they are and what they can accomplish,' she says.

Each of the students at PPSS may have an intellectual disability, but it does not define them. While each student will gain many valuable skills during their years at school, their greatest accomplishment is to possess a strong sense of their own self-worth and potential. For any child, at any school, having such belief in their own ability is essential as they step forward in life.

~~~~~~~~

One easy way to see proof of performance at PPSS is to visit the building which some staff call the House of Independence, a house on school grounds where students learn independent living skills.

'I wanted our children to have a place where they could practise a wide variety of skills that they need at home, in the actual environment,' Bella explains.

But in Port Melbourne, an attractive two-bedroom house could easily fetch $700 000. How did PPSS afford it? 'It was free,' Bella explains, indicating the plaque, which lists the many donors, headlined by the major contributor, Thiess Construction Company.

Bella made an art of asking for things the school needed. As principal, she asked early, often, always—for anything and everything. And she asked everyone.

'I don't find it difficult,' she insists. 'People have so much that they can contribute, and they want to! Besides, I'm not asking for myself, but for these deserving children.'

~~~~~~~~

In practice: The House of Independence

Chris Edmonds stands in the centre of the kitchen and eyes the perfectly swept floor critically. She opens one of the kitchen cupboards and pulls out a plastic container of rolled oats. Then she judiciously pours a generous helping of the cereal onto the floor. Chris sprinkles more oats near the bench and drops a spotted trail all around the kitchen table.

'Very Hansel and Gretel,' she nods with satisfaction, before placing the oats container back in the pantry and heading down the hall to the bedroom, which she proceeds to ransack. Chris tosses pillows onto the floor, pulls out neatly tucked sheets, rumples the twin doonas. She pauses to admire her handiwork. 'Perfect!'

Chris's apparent madness is pure method. 'It's impossible to tidy a house that is already clean,' she explains, as a knock at the front door indicates her students have arrived.

'Good morning, everyone!' Chris greets the small band of teenagers.

This is an independent living class at PPSS—a class designed to teach skills that are both basic and yet crucial to growing up. From working on domestic chores like meal preparation, setting the table and cleaning the house, to personal care such as putting on deodorant and shaving, these students have the luxury of learning home skills in a genuine house. PPSS serves a wide-ranging community. Some students here are from middle-class or wealthy families, while others live in commission housing. For all, having a clean, well-stocked house on school grounds is an example of what a typical home can include, as well as a teaching resource.

'Don't forget to wash your hands,' Chris reminds the students. 'Then come back and choose an apron from the hooks, and we'll get ready to work. Today we need volunteers to sweep the floor, make the beds, iron, clean the mirror, and generally tidy up before we can get to our cooking lesson.'

But as the teenagers return from the bathroom, assistant teacher Ben Lorenz isn't satisfied with one or two of the students. 'Hey, Dan, did you dry your hands, mate?'

'On my pants,' Dan responds sheepishly.

'Not good enough,' Ben shakes his head, gesturing for Dan to use a towel.

That's one reason the very first lesson on this day concerns personal grooming. The focus is on brushing teeth and hair. As always at PPSS, the arts are part and parcel of teaching; the students will practise the skills through singing.

'Is everyone ready?' Chris asks, as the students assemble at the kitchen table. She turns on a CD player. 'Boris, are you ready?' she consults a tiny chef perched on her left hand.

'Hello!' responds the puppet, with a wave of his whisk. 'Now who wants to sing about Jim?'

A chorus of 'Me!' greets that question. The students love Boris, and the song about a young man who didn't have a bath for 26 days. Chris distributes dry face washers for the children to use at their table as they sing and pretend to wash. With enthusiasm, they proceed to give themselves a pretend bath, which culminates in miming pulling out the plug and having the water glug down the drain.

Music isn't the only branch of the arts employed at the House of Independence. In virtually every class at PPSS, the arts can be found in the foreground, the background, or both. Consider the walls of the kitchen and dining room, which display more than a dozen canvases of vibrant fruits painted by students. The mixed-media oils include the names of the fruits, either painted or collaged in a mismatched collection of letters vaguely reminiscent of Hollywood's version of a ransom note. The children's navy aprons, stencilled with chefs' hats, and the table in the kitchen area, which is stencilled with images of knives, forks and spoons, are other projects completed in Ross Denby's art room.

Learning to prepare healthy cuisine is another element of this personal development class.

'This term we are focusing on cooking with lots of vegetables,' Chris reminds the students. 'What have we made, class?'

'Pizza!'

'Our gourmet pizzas, yum! And we made soup, remember? Pumpkin with potato and leek. What else?'

'Fried rice!' answers one girl.

'That's right, with "sorry" sauce. Who was it who called soy sauce, "sorry sauce"? That's how I write it on my shopping list now!' Chris says.

Fostering communication is a key goal in every class at PPSS. Around the kitchen and throughout the house, laminated Picture Communication Symbols are everywhere, so that students who don't read—as well as those who do—know where to find things.

Later, after the students have finished all of their chores, including carefully sweeping up the last of the scattered oats, a student named Poppy conducts a tour of the house. Poppy's speech is excellent and she clearly relishes showing off the cottage. Walking from the kitchen into a central hallway she waves to the left, gesturing to a room equipped with a computer, 'That's the study.' Then, further down the hallway, 'And this is the bedroom,' she explains. 'I like the posters,' she says shyly, looking at the magazine pictures of stars like Hannah Montana that are stuck to the bedroom walls.

Poppy points to the twin beds. 'We make them,' she tells me. 'I like to put a teddy bear on the pillow, for cuddles.'

———~~~———

Perhaps the most visual, obvious example of proof of performance is to watch the transition class in action at the Short Break Cafe. The service, food and attention are such that you might feel like you are meeting a friend for a coffee in any main street restaurant.

———~~~———

In practice: Lessons from the Short Break Cafe

The air is fragrant with the smell of sizzling onions and homemade bread. While one teen carefully dices zucchini, another smooths a table cloth and a third places a small vase of flowers on another table.

In the corner, a student is tinkering with the base of a standing fan, as transition teacher Jacqui Chalmers pulls the latest batch of scones out of the oven. She studies the tray with a critical air, then gingerly picks up one scone and raps it against the bench. Thud.

'Who made the scones?'

With a sheepish expression, Xavier raises his hand.

'How many times did you knead them?' Jacqui quizzes him.

'I dunno. Ten or fifteen?'

'Too many, mate. Just a couple. Otherwise, instead of light and fluffy, you get bricks.' Jacqui dumps the scones into a bowl and pushes them aside for the students to chew through later. She gives Xavier an encouraging grin. 'Okay, get going. Still time to make another batch before we open.'

Xavier shakes his head, as he measures flour, adds cream and lemonade to prepare the scones. 'Why's everybody picking on my scones?' he grumbles good-naturedly under his breath, but Jacqui is unapologetic.

'You've got to get it right,' she responds, before moving on to check on the progress of the vegetarian 'sausage' rolls, the zucchini muffins and the preparation of the cafe.

'Good job, Cameron—you've diced those carrots finely. Hey, Deb. What about the order sheets? Can you go photocopy another 50 for me? Declan! We need more cutlery, mate. Okay, guys, what are we sitting down for? We have serviettes that need to be out. Move it everybody, we open in 15 minutes!'

As the hubbub kicks up a notch, Jacqui's eyes swerve to the student who is still fixing the electric fan base.

'John!'

'I'm fixing it,' he protests, holding up the tool in mock surrender.

'Put down the screwdriver and step away. It's time to get ready for the customers.'

John shrugs, turns aside reluctantly. Then, he's back at the fan, apparently sucked in by some invisible centrifugal force.

'Off you go,' she tells him firmly, as she escorts him out of the cafe, past a group of teachers who are bustling in.

Morning rush at the Short Break Cafe is underway.

What began as a transition class to teach a raft of useful skills using a 'real world' model has morphed into a Wednesday morning ritual eagerly awaited by PPSS staff. Teachers and administrators flock to the cafe in the heart of the school for a coffee, along with a snack for morning tea.

Location isn't the Short Break Cafe's only advantage. Proximity might prompt one visit, but what has ensured repeat business is good food at a fair price.

Each week the cafe opens not only to teachers, but to students. Some younger children are brought here by their teacher and assistant teacher to practise dining-out skills, like sitting still in a chair and trying not to create a mess while eating, as many parents cite being able to take their child to a restaurant as a significant goal.

But on this particular morning, in addition to the clatter and chatter of the cafe, there is the unmistakable whir of a fan. But John is conspicuously absent. And the standing fan? It stands silent, neglected. This sound emanates from just outside the cafe, as does the clear, unmistakable voice of Jacqui Chalmers. 'Just one more kilometre. You're almost there.'

It turns out this fan is located inside the front wheel of an exercise bike John is pedalling hard. With one last vigorous push, he completes his goal and hops off. Without a backwards glance, John saunters into the cafe and assumes his duties as a waiter.

'We try to make discipline fit the offence,' Jacqui explains after John's gone. 'John is a great kid but sometimes he doesn't listen. He has a lot of excess energy and we need to harness that. He's also obsessed with tools and fixing things, but doesn't always know when to stop and can wind up fixing something, only to break it again.'

John's love of tools and tinkering is so well known at PPSS that he's been unofficially granted his own 'office'—a closet off the transition classroom where he stores some of his tools and tinkers in his spare time.

'Taking a turn on the exercise bike burns off energy,' Jacqui continues. 'That calms him down and is a lot more meaningful than sending him to the principal's office.' She pauses. 'Besides, sending him there didn't work anyway, because he *loved* it. He had a chance to chat to staff!' she laughs. 'Instead, we now treat going there as a reward. If he earns 10 "ticks" in a day, he gets to spend time with our assistant principal, which is a big incentive.'

Back inside the cafe, John isn't the only busy waiter. Another student is taking the order of a prep teacher.

'Would you like jam and cream with your scones?' asks Wendy.

Wendy is another PPSS success story. She greets customers with a steady gaze and a clear, confident voice. It's hard to believe this self-assured young woman was once so shy she couldn't look anyone in the eye and found it nearly impossible to speak. As has been true for many students, the practice of taking orders at the cafe was part of the remedy.

Wendy's first big breakthrough came during a different program of the transition class, using one of the MP3 players Jacqui had purchased for the students to share. Jacqui says she uses the latest technology as much as possible because it is highly motivating for teenagers.

On this occasion, the students had been asked to do some recording, but Wendy was perplexed to discover that her machine didn't work.

'I can't hear my voice,' she whispered.

'No-one can,' Jacqui explained gently, to Wendy's astonishment. The thrill of using an iPod® was a great incentive to practise and Wendy found her voice.

'Two scones with jam and cream, please,' Wendy calls out, as she hands an order sheet through the window to the kitchen. Wendy can read and write, but not all of the transition students can. Yet they can all wait tables because the order forms are printed with pictures as well as words.

Pictures also adorn the outside of the kitchen cupboards, signifying where the dishes, cutlery and saucepans are stored.

The restaurant program is designed to teach a variety of important skills, including maths. One student stands at the register, counting the day's take.

'We make sure we turn a profit,' Jacqui explains, 'just like any successful business. The kids are motivated by how much the cafe can earn, and when we go to the shops every Wednesday morning, they check to see what's on special. For example, we used to serve a fresh fruit salad, but discovered that was too expensive. Items on our current menu are tasty, but also economical.'

At the end of each term, students who took part in the cafe program are taken out for lunch to let them experience eating at a cafe or restaurant and being waited on.

Occupational therapy is also included. From kneading bread to dicing garlic and zucchini, students master complex fine motor skills. While many specialist and mainstream schools offer 'pull out' or 'push in' occupational therapy—either taking a child out of the classroom, or working one-on-one in the class, respectively—PPSS found that having an occupational therapist help design the class curriculum and then work with all the students as a group was a better use of resources. PPSS occupational therapist Jo White worked with Jacqui to figure out how to weave fine motor activities into the program. On Wednesdays, she and another occupational therapist, Skye Purtill, are on hand to watch and assist as those skills are put into action. The program is revised and changes are made, both on the spot and over time.

Opening hours are over for the day. The cheerful cafe is slowly being turned back into a classroom. Tablecloths are folded and it's time for the day's welcome reward—a chance to eat the leftovers, including the not-half-bad-with-cream-and-jam brick scones.

Wii® love school

'The iPod® is just one example of how we use current technology to teach our students,' Jacqui explains, as she gestures to printouts of Wii® scores that are plastered on the walls of the cafe/classroom. Clearly the students have had a ball.

'We play Wii® tennis, bowling and skiing, but it's not just about the skills embedded in the game. We find the students are motivated to calculate their scores, as well as graph their progress over time—and there we are doing maths again,' Jacqui smiles.

The students also participate in a partnership program with the St Kilda Youth Service in which they are making an animated movie. From drawing to making props, from writing a screenplay to learning about stop animation, from film-making to photography, the program is exciting as well as educational. And the storyline of the students' project is predictably teen-friendly.

'It's a movie about a truck crashing into the Montague Street bridge,' Jacqui explains. 'There's a ghost train. Johnny Depp is our main character.'

Jacqui constantly keeps in mind the age of her students as she plans the program. While younger students at PPSS do a school production every year in front of a live audience complete with costumes and music, Jacqui understands that teenagers—especially young men—aren't enthusiastic about that.

'So instead of that, we did a TV show. We worked on our script, content and recording all year. We did our own version of a *Better Homes and Gardens* program and everyone learned a lot about home crafts and cookery, in addition to television. The project required oral and written communication, but the kids just loved it because it was TV. They did a fantastic job,' Jacqui says.

Looking around at the comfortable, secure and confident students, it is easy to see that they are close to being ready for prime time. Moving on from school. Finding jobs. Finding independence. Finding their way. From the Short Break Cafe, it's just a short step to the real world. And these students can't wait.

Conclusion

In 2011, Port Phillip Special School underwent a diagnostic school review. This review is part of Department of Education and Early Childhood Development (DEECD) accountability process and occurs every four years. The entire staff and the school council were involved in analysing how PPSS operates on every level. The results confirmed what those at the school already knew: their Visual and Performing Art Curriculum (VPAC) and integrated services infrastructure is working.

To confirm that the school is achieving measurable positive results for its students is heartening, but PPSS continues to strive to be the best it possibly can, to explore ways to innovate and improve, and to maintain a strong focus on staff professional development. The staff's extraordinary dedication, skills and commitment to staying at the forefront of educational and therapeutic best practice are key to the success of the school.

As we conclude this particular account of the development of PPSS, it is difficult to imagine the school without its House of Independence, which got a brand-new kitchen garden in 2011, created by the children and staff. Or without the pool, where students make major gains in strength, coordination and confidence thanks to the hydrotherapy program. Without the 2.3-million-dollar performing arts centre, home to the school's magical performances. Without the recording studio, dance studio, gym, instruments and equipment. We hope that by charting the journey of PPSS, from its humble beginnings to the substantial institution it is today, this book will inspire its readers to consider how possible it is to create change in special needs education.

PPSS is unusual, but it does not need to be. The approaches to teaching can be replicated anywhere, by any school. PPSS is at the forefront of education reform, and can serve as a model of what can—and what should—be accomplished. PPSS has demonstrated that a fully-serviced, integrated approach works, and that an arts-based curriculum is a powerful tool for reaching children with special needs.

The school's remarkable Visual and Performing Arts Curriculum holds promise, not just for children here, but for all students. As Bella Irlicht said, of the UNESCO conference she and her colleagues attended in 2006, 'Everyone was talking about the arts. But no-one was talking about how the arts can be used for children who have an intellectual disability. But that was what we were doing, at PPSS.'

The next step is clear. VPAC and the integrated services approach should be used more widely. If recent developments in the field of brain science tell us anything, it is that music, art, dance and drama are powerful tools for reaching children who have an intellectual disability. But without integrated services the effect is limited. I believe we should pay PPSS the greatest compliment, and strive to emulate what they are doing. And I hope this book will show educators, parents and policymakers how it can be done, and why it is so important: for our children—all of them—and for the future.

Sara James

A note from Bella Irlicht AM

••

Every organisation is only as good as its weakest link. Our links were strong and tight. From the earliest days, we were supported by an extraordinary group of men and women—leaders in the realms of arts, sport, media, education, government and academia. PPSS has been fortunate indeed to have had brilliant, accomplished men and women who gave us their all—their money, their time, their ideas and their insight. They provided the scaffolding upon which we built a magnificent school. There is an old saying, that, 'If I have seen farther, it is by standing on the shoulders of giants.' PPSS has stood on the shoulders of Titans ... and I want to thank them here.

With so many talented, big-hearted men and women to thank, I hardly know where to begin. I will approach this both chronologically and by grouping our many friends according to their specialties.

I must begin with Kathy Anasta, who held my hand from the first day I walked into the school. For 20 years she was not only the school's business manager, but my friend, my confidante and my right brain: she knew what I was thinking before I did. When we started we had $8000 in the bank and no equipment. With a lot of brainstorming and a lot of planning, together we embarked on the journey. Nothing was too much trouble for Kathy. She was the one who developed our school magazine from a sheet of paper to the high standard it became, and importantly, she recognised the power of branding for the school. In 20 years not once did she let me down. I know it sounds clichéd but she was the wind beneath my wings and we soared together.

Next, I'd like to thank Leo Lipp. Our relationship with Leo began when I called in at Photomation, a local production company, unannounced, and met one of the partners, Leo. I told Leo I'd seen a video they produced for a fashion show, and wanted to know if they could produce something similar for our school. He told me it had cost

$20 000 to produce and asked me what our budget was. Gulp. We didn't have one. I thanked him for his time and got ready to leave.

To my surprise and delight, he extended his hand, smiled, and said, 'Let's not worry about the budget now.' He went on to produce our logo, letterhead and several dynamic videos. This meant I could take the school with me, so to speak, when I was sourcing the corporate dollar. Leo became a friend and supporter of PPSS.

Events and entertainment

Given that I had the tools, I could now think about putting on events to showcase the school—to 'friend raise' and fundraise. The secret of being a leader is knowing what you don't know. I realised I didn't have the expertise or the contacts to put on the kind of functions I dreamed of for our school. I needed professionals.

The very first entertainer and television personality to champion our cause was Johnny Young, from the original *Young Talent Time*. Johnny was a patron of the school from 1989 and hosted many of our early fundraising events.

Television personality Glenn Ridge, for many years the host of *Sale of the Century*, emceed countless times, was featured in our videos, and gave tirelessly. A small note: Glenn tells me he would practise saying 'No' to me, but in the event, would always relent! Thanks, Glenn, for saying 'When, where, and how much do you need?' instead of 'No'. Your generosity of spirit set the tone of our school.

Bettina Spivakovsky, of Upfront Entertainment, had contacts everywhere, from performers to emcees to experts in the technical world, and her professionalism is matched only by her big heart. We immediately got to work, and she helped us to produce the most amazing events, from a formal ball to football breakfasts and racing lunches.

Paul Davies, from Events Australia, also made a huge commitment to the school. Here we had two people, in companies which competed head-to-head in the marketplace, combining forces and resources to assist our school. We couldn't be more grateful.

We've been fortunate to have many supporters from the world of entertainment. Singers Mike Brady—famous for 'Up There Cazaly'—and Bruce Woodley of The Seekers have been amazing.

I would also like to thank Susan Cooper, who helped the school to organise the world-class International Symposium on Re-imagining Special Education through Arts Education and Arts Therapy in 2008.

Education and academia

Renowned education consultant Pam Russell has been my mentor and guide over the years. Pam provided the nuts and bolts which were crucial to the building of a new school. She played a pivotal role in the shaping and designing of our arts-based curriculum, as well as the arts conference, and was a key figure in ensuring that PPSS's innovative curriculum became known internationally. Pam gave from the heart, and her work for PPSS was pro bono.

Pam introduced us to a former Dean of Education and Training at RMIT University, Emeritus Professor Martin Comte OAM, whose talents are extraordinary, and who was happy to share them with us.

Dr Judith Paphazy, a renowned psychologist and writer, played a pivotal role in supporting our parent population. She ran many classes and group workshops for the school, which were very well attended by parents, who benefited from her wisdom, knowledge and plain common sense. Over many years, Judith has been a tower of strength to parents, to staff, and particularly to me.

Betty Levy, the school psychologist and Ros Jennings, our social worker, helped me set up structures within the school, especially the integrated services model, which continued to evolve and improve until we got it right. Our dream was to have the first fully-serviced specialist school in Australia with an arts-based curriculum. Both of these highly professional people supported all aspects of the dream, and promoted the dreamer.

Professor Brian Caldwell, former Dean of Education at the University of Melbourne, understood my vision from the beginning. He encouraged me to look beyond the school, beyond Victoria, indeed beyond Australia. Brian lectured around the world, and always used our school as an example of best practice. When you have someone of his calibre promoting the principal and the school, people take you seriously. Brian helped us achieve our dream of taking what we'd learned internationally. It was during one such international trip—a Women in Leadership tour in England, which he hosted—that I first came across the literature on the fully-serviced school. It was a revelation. It helped me put my ideas about education into context, and being able to discuss these ideas with Brian was worth more than gold.

Also from the University of Melbourne, Dr Laurie Drysdale and Professor David Gurr enthusiastically promoted the school, invested their time into conducting longitudinal studies of the progress of the school and helped us document our progress.

University of Melbourne Dean of Education Professor Field Rickards and Associate Dean Professor Patrick Griffin have also taken a keen interest in our school and have endorsed our work.

I met Graeme Meadows, education consultant and former principal of Dandenong South Primary School, many years ago and he has been a mentor, colleague and a friend. He has served on so many occasions as a mirror, offering up alternative ways to deal with issues and situations. He often helped me clarify my vision.

I got an enormous amount of support from the highest echelons in the education department of Victoria, including former ministers and deputy secretaries. I'd like to thank former education ministers and secretaries, Phillip Gude, Dr Jeff Dunstan and Geoff Spring. I also had the privilege of working with Darrell Fraser, John Allman and Ian Claridge. Darrell Fraser, who was the director of schools and one of the key people in the department, supported our conference totally. He, John and Ian attended many of our functions and have always taken a keen interest in the development and growth of the school. They've all supported the vision and been amazing in their commitment.

At PPSS, we had 60 people on staff with a unique combination of talents, skills and knowledge, including special educators, therapists, assistants and support staff. Each member of staff made a significant contribution to the overall direction and vision. They were passionate about the school and deeply invested in helping each student reach his or her full potential. To my staff I will always be eternally grateful.

As just one example, Jeanette Liddle, a well-known ballerina, popped into my office one day to ask how she could help. She volunteered to begin our dance program, which is still going strong today. Our children thank her.

Sports and volunteers

We've had many extraordinary volunteers, but few who've had the reach and created the ripple effects of Maureen Hafey, who was instrumental in starting the PPSS choir. She had choir uniforms made, and then invited the choir to sing for 1000 people at the Grand Final Lunch at the Crown Casino.

Maureen, the wife of former Richmond Football Club coach Tom Hafey, encouraged others in the world of Australian Rules football to support our school, including Mary Williams and Carolyn Stubbs.

Maureen, Mary and Carolyn had extensive networks of contacts in the football community, which they generously shared with us. These ladies gave their all, and then asked, 'What else can we do?'

Along with former senior banker Michael Darcy, Maureen, Mary and Carolyn became the heart of our football committee, which put on a series of high-profile events for school. Thanks to Greg Moore, we were always well looked after at the Crown Entertainment Complex, where we hosted these events.

Many people in the football fraternity helped us, and the 'five greatest coaches' joined forces to support the vision. I'd like to thank famous players and coaches David Parkin, Tommy Hafey, Kevin Sheedy, Ron Barassi and the late Allan Jeans for this support.

I had known David Parkin, former captain of Hawthorn Football Club and AFL coach, for many years. In 1975, he was my lecturer in physical education for special needs children, at the University of Melbourne. David has supported every function we've had. He's always contributed and volunteered. He's been a guest speaker, and committed a great deal of time, energy and resources to support the school. David's sense of community and his generosity are second to none.

Footballers aren't the only athletes who have supported our students. From the racing fraternity, Des O'Keefe and many famous jockeys and trainers have helped to raise money for our school.

Friends

There has been a series of concentric circles, as friends I've known and friends I've met along the way have laboured together to build our school.

Dr Jamie Robertson was our family dentist. He was also instrumental in helping to start the dental clinic at PPSS. Jamie got support from Dental Health Services Victoria, as well as from companies, such as Colgate.

Sue Jamieson has volunteered for the last 20 years and worked on every function, bringing family and friends in tow. She deserves a medal. She was also a member of our school foundation, which was set up by lawyer Phillip Jones. Moreover, Sue also helped me set up the Friends of PPSS (FOPPSS). Our school council, meanwhile, has supported our vision under the leadership of Michelle Blannin for many years. Don Chisholm has served on the council for more than 20 years, offering sound legal advice.

There are many parents who have been incredibly supportive. Christine and Peter Barro were heavily involved in the school and its community. Together we shared an incredible journey. Ross Illingworth must also get special mention. He introduced me to people who were fundamental to the growth of the school. He also supported me as a leader, and was instrumental in nominating me for the Equity Trustees Not for Profit CEO of the Year Award.

Through my involvement with Equity Trustees, I met Ken Berry who happened to be involved with two other philanthropic organisations: the Independent Order of Odd Fellows and the Newsboys Foundation. Both organisations made significant contributions to our school.

Ross also introduced me to Ken Moffatt, who over dinner pledged $20 000 to our cause. The cheque was on my desk before I got to work the next morning.

Philanthropy

PPSS has been blessed with the support of many extraordinary trusts and foundations.

At the Pratt Foundation, Heloise Waislitz, Sam Lipsky AM and Ian Allen OAM have been extraordinary. Heloise, Sam and Ian followed the old advice that rather than offering people a meal, you should teach them how to fish. They sent me to a course in philanthropy, which they paid for, at Indiana University. As well as funds for various projects, they provided the leverage for the building of the arts centre. They supported my vision and took a keen interest not only in giving funds to the school, but in monitoring the progress of the school and the project they supported.

There are no words to express my sincere thanks to Heloise, Sam and Ian for their trust and commitment to the school and to me personally.

I also would like to extend my thanks to those at the Helen McPherson Smith Trust, the Jack Brockhoff Foundation, Variety and the Invergowrie Foundation, as well as to Dame Elisabeth Murdoch AC, DBE and her granddaughter Penny Fowler. I have valued their friendship, their trust and their support.

Conclusion

A lot of times people working in special needs education are supported by groups who have some tie to disabilities, but this has not been the case with PPSS.

PPSS represents a kaleidoscope of events and people. We were the only school that had an independent foundation, a unique curriculum and a community of staff and parents who were totally aligned. We had ties in every sector of the community and a huge circle of friends who have all contributed to creating an extraordinary school.

It has been a wonderful journey, but without my husband Michael and my children Robert, Naomi and James, it may have been too difficult for me. They were my strength and my support. Collectively and individually, they were totally committed to assisting with events, special projects and the development of the school. More importantly, they selflessly allowed me to devote a significant amount of my time and energy to others. I thank them with all my heart.

A note from Sam Lipski AM, CEO of the Pratt Foundation

The legendary American baseball player and coach Yogi Berra had a way with words. Of his many sayings, my favourite is: 'It's déjà vu all over again' (Berra 2002, p. 137). So it is with looking back through the files to trace how the Pratt Foundation's partnership with the Port Phillip Specialist School began and developed.

Reading Bella Irlicht's 'Principal's Report' in the 1998 school magazine, there it was. Said Bella: 'As I reflect on the past 10 years that I have been privileged to lead this dynamic organisation, I feel excited about the enormity of the paradigm shift that we have managed so well.'

Yes, that's right. 'The paradigm shift.' Sound familiar? Reading that phrase, as I did, during the same weekend, in September 2010, that Prime Minister Julia Gillard announced a new ministry and 'the new paradigm' in parliament and government, merely confirmed what I already knew. In 1998, Bella was ahead of her time.

For one thing, she had used the phrase correctly. Without spin. In the very next paragraph she explained clearly what she meant by paradigm shift. 'The change from a small special development school to a large specialist school has created many more opportunities for children within our area and has given us the opportunity to showcase and lead the way in special education in provision of curriculum, a range of specialist services, and, in particular, support for parents.'

But Bella was already looking beyond the 'shift' to the 'vision'. Thus, towards the end of her 1998 report, she referred to the expanding range of service providers who would ensure that 'our vision of the fully-serviced school is achieved'.

Which is about when and where the Pratt Foundation came into the picture. Chair of the Pratt Foundation, Heloise Waislitz, had taken up the philanthropic tradition and leadership which her parents, Jeanne and

Richard Pratt, had developed. Some time in the spring of 1998, Heloise asked me and Ian Allen, my co-trustee at the Pratt Foundation, to join her on a field visit to PPSS. Heloise's interest had arisen from her close friendship with Gina Rose. In 1998, Gina's four-year-old son, Harley, who had severe disabilities, was a student in the PPSS's Early Education Centre. Gina was passionate about seeking support for the school.

It didn't take us long to see why. The school, its teachers, children and parents, had an immediate impact on any visitor. It was akin to a bodily sensation, and it certainly left an emotional imprint. Anybody who had ever been involved with children with significant disabilities was at once aware that the skills and dedication of the teachers, combined with the range of services on offer, from speech pathology to sensory processing, and from music to art, offered hope far beyond the usual.

And, of course, Bella was far beyond the usual. A force of nature. You know those forces when you come across them. She was reason enough for me to know, and for Heloise to confirm to me the moment we had left the school, that we were going to support her work.

From that first visit, which happened just a few weeks after I became the Pratt Foundation's Chief Executive, I began referring to the 'Port Phillip Special School'—because I thought it was obvious that it was 'special' in every sense of the word. It took me a few years to realise that I wasn't referring to the school by its correct 'specialist' title.

After a second visit to PPSS, during which Bella outlined the major steps which lay ahead to fulfil the vision for the fully-serviced school, we agreed that she would submit four funding proposals to the Pratt Foundation. As outlined in her letter of 18 December 1998 and the accompanying submission, the four requests were for: a director of integrated services, to be funded over three years at $120000; a manager for a training and research centre, to be funded over three years at $105000; an adaptive technology resource centre, needing $145000 over three years; and enhanced learning programs, at $140000 over three years.

Guided by Bella's submission and discussion with Ian Allen, I decided to recommend the grant for the director of integrated services. In a memo to Heloise on 28 January 1999, I wrote: 'I believe this school is a first-class and far-sighted project which is pointing the way with its concept of the fully-serviced school … It is a "leader" as Bella Irlicht is a leader.'

In addition, I said I believed that each of us associated with the Pratt Foundation would find it 'personally rewarding' to be involved with the school as it grew and developed into a model for others.

I offered three reasons for my preference for offering the grant for a director of integrated services.

Firstly, I wrote, when there was a choice between funding a person who can make a difference and the centre or activity that person would lead, 'we should aim to invest in the person'.

Secondly, as Bella had explained, the director of integrated services was the critical appointment which would enable all the other planned activities 'to get underway and be productive'.

And, very importantly for a foundation which always has to worry what happens when its grant money runs out, Bella had made it clear she intended the position to be 'self-funding in three years'. 'Not only does it mean that the level of support diminishes over three years ($60000, $40000 and $20000) but it shows a business-like approach,' I wrote.

After further discussion, Heloise approved the memo, and Ian signed off in agreement, subject to PPSS outlining the director's performance criteria. On 4 March 1999 I phoned Bella to tell her the good news, and on 11 March I wrote 'formally' confirming the grant. Bella replied to Heloise on 15 March, thanking her warmly, and saying that 'the school community was absolutely ecstatic with the news'.

It took a while for PPSS to find the director they were looking for. But when they did in 2000, his appointment was both a statement and a turning point. That Professor Carl Parsons, Professor of Child Language Disorders at La Trobe University, who had an international reputation in developing treatment programs for children with disabilities, was ready to take on the job spoke volumes. In a conversation shortly after his appointment I asked the obvious question: Why would a professor of education come to a small school? I vividly recall his answer: 'I've been teaching teachers and doing research about special education for 25 years. This is a chance, not just to teach, but to do it.' And do it he did. Over the next decade or so, Carl's work with students and staff was pivotal.

For us, that was the beginning. Gina Rose, full of life and energy and love for her Harley, had been the parent who had brought the Pratt Foundation to PPSS. Tragically, Gina was also the parent who, in her untimely death in a road accident two years later, led us to our next major project at the school. Heloise was deeply shocked and saddened by her friend's death and she wanted to honour her friend in a way that would be meaningful for Gina's family, especially for Harley, and for the school. She met with Bella and asked how she could help—which is how we learned about Bella's dream to teach children with disabilities, such as Harley, through a centre for the visual and performing arts.

Why the arts? As Bella put it in one of her letters to potential supporters in May 2004, after she had convinced us that it mattered: 'Changes in educational practice around the world see arts in education as a new priority because the arts leads to success for children with disabilities ... and success is what we want for our children.' Success for our children. Four very powerful words that drove Bella and all around her. Four words that kept recurring throughout our partnership with the school.

During 2003 and 2004, Ian and I met with Bella, her staff and Paul Hede the architect. We had further discussions with Heloise and reviewed the plans. Although the meetings were rewarding, indeed often inspirational, working out how we would help fund the project did not always go smoothly. It was clear that the centre would have to be a $1-million-plus undertaking. But as needs and plans changed, costs inevitably began to creep up on Bella's vision. Eventually we decided that as we had agreed to be 'the funder of last resort', we had to ask Bella 'diplomatically' not to incur any further costs without first checking each new increase or extra fitting with us. Bella took our 'request' in her stride, cheerfully explaining that although she was aware of the growing costs, she was 'an educator, not a builder'.

But, of course, she was very much a builder. So, having sorted out an agreed balance between her 'grand vision' and what could be done within the budget, in March 2004 we agreed to provide an initial grant of $300000 towards the centre's capital costs. We did so on the understanding that the school would try to raise the balance, which at that time we estimated would be around $1 million, from government and other sources.

We knew that was a big ask. While Heloise had made it clear that we were prepared, if necessary, to pay for the total costs, we thought it was such an important undertaking that government investment was justified. We explained our view on the importance of using our philanthropic funding, not as an end in itself, but as 'leverage' for government and other donors.

Bella and her supporters listened, really listened, and become increasingly professional in their fundraising, particularly under Ian Allen's tutelage. They took the project to a new level. They learned about 'leverage' as they went, attracted the $1 million from the Victorian government, and sourced additional corporate and philanthropic support from Qantas, Variety, the Jack and Robert Smorgon Families and Equity Trustees.

So on that unforgettable evening, 14 September 2005, the Victorian Deputy Premier, John Thwaites, and the Minister for Educational Services, Jacinta Allen, opened the Gina Rose Visual and Performing Arts Centre. Heloise spoke about Gina. Bella spoke about her vision and the story. The children of PPSS sang. Parents and families were caught between tears and joy. We all were.

For Bella the story continued just a month later when, on 11 October, she received the Not for Profit CEO of the Year Award at the Rod Laver Arena. Presented by the Equity Trustees, the award recognised 'exceptional leadership that embodies a vision and has the clear capacity to translate this into reality'. Bella was chosen from a field of some 100 candidates around Australia, many of them well-known public figures. Quite a coup. It was my privilege, as one of Bella's referees, to represent the Pratt Foundation and sit with Bella and her family as we waited, uncertain and anxious, for the announcement. When it came, Bella grabbed my arm and held on in disbelief. A special moment in a special year.

Since then, the Pratt Foundation has continued its relationship with the school. It has been a most rewarding one for all of us. I have to say, however, that looking back over more than a decade it has been a one-sided partnership. After all, we have received far more in return than anything we may have given.

Glossary

Allied health assistant An individual who has had training (usually a one- or two-year part-time certificate level course) to provide therapeutic assistance and support to clients under the direct supervision of an occupational therapist, physiotherapist, speech–language pathologist or other qualified health care professional. Allied health assistants can provide support only for routine procedures.

Antecedent–behaviour–consequence (ABC) A theory used in applied behaviour analysis (see below) that indicates that in order to alter a behaviour it is necessary either to change what happens immediately before the behaviour (the antecedent) or immediately after the behaviour (the consequence).

Applied behaviour analysis (ABA) (also known as discrete trial training) ABA therapy, developed in the United States by Ivar Lovaas, is an intensive one-on-one therapy used in the treatment of autism spectrum disorders. The therapist teaches a skill by breaking it down into small parts; much repetition is required and reinforcement is provided by positive feedback. ABA focuses on observable behaviours, and was designed to eliminate negative and destructive behaviours and to encourage positive ones. The therapy has its proponents and detractors. Critics allege that it teaches students to respond only to certain types of commands and requests, that it can lead to robotic-type responses and that students trained with this technique show little initiation. Another criticism has been that people used as trainers often undergo only a one- or two-day training program and then refer to themselves as 'ABA therapists'. There are numerous variations on this approach, such as 'the new ABA' and the 'verbal behaviour program'.

Arts therapy The use of art therapy, dance therapy, drama therapy and music therapy to change either physical, psychological, emotional, social or behavioural difficulties.

Asperger's syndrome A form of autism spectrum disorder. Asperger's syndrome is characterised by difficulties in social interaction, repetitive behaviour and often a unique interest and/or competence in one specific area. It is thought that many people with Asperger's syndrome have an IQ in the average or above-average range (Gallagher & Gallagher 2002); most people with Asperger's syndrome are verbal.

Auslan Australian Sign Language, originally designed for use by deaf people.

Autism spectrum disorder (ASD) A neurological- and genetic-based disability. Appears in a child's first three years of life, and is characterised by difficulty in social interactions, being non-verbal or having difficulty with speech and communication, problems understanding others and repetitive and ritualistic behaviours. People with ASD may also have challenging behaviours and sensory difficulties. Disorders are often associated with intellectual disability. ASD includes autism, Asperger's syndrome and pervasive development disorder not otherwise specified.

Big book An enlarged version of a simple book, illustrated and with large text, designed for beginning readers or to be read aloud to students by a staff member.

Early Education Program (EEP) An educational service offered at PPSS and a few other specialist schools in Victoria for children with disabilities in the age range of two years and eight months to four years and eight months. These programs are similar to Early Childhood Intervention Services (funded by the Victorian state government to support children with disabilities from birth to school entry), but are not funded as such and thus use a different name.

Fully-serviced school A school which has a multidisciplinary team on-site to meet the complicated, diverse needs of students and their families. As articulated in Joy Dryfoos' (1994) book *Full-Service Schools*, such a facility 'integrates education, medical, social, and/or human services that are beneficial to meeting the needs of children and youth and their families on school grounds or in locations which are easily accessible'. PPSS is a fully-serviced school.

Health hustle Mandatory morning physical activity for all students and staff at PPSS. This program is offered to foster fitness and a healthy lifestyle, and as a preparation for daily educational activities. Most staff and students engage in walking or jogging around the school block. Others students may swim or participate in yoga or other physical activities as decided by the Integrated Services Committee.

House of Independence A house on the PPSS property where students practise and learn independent living skills such as cooking, cleaning, making beds, washing clothes, and so on.

Hydrotherapy A therapy involving exercise in a heated pool, under the instruction of a qualified instructor or physiotherapist, designed to relax and/or strengthen muscles and improve body tone and function.

Inclusion kindergarten A program in which children with an intellectual or physical disability are integrated into a typical kindergarten classroom. PPSS has access to this type of program for some of its Early Education Program students.

Individual Education Plan (IEP) (also known as Individual Learning Plan) Mandated by the state of Victoria for all children and young people with any disability, an Individual Education Plan is a written plan developed in collaboration between a student's parents and his or her school, to help determine and prioritise the needs of the student. Each student's IEP identifies the student's key academic goals and explains how teachers, therapists and other support staff will help the student achieve the set goals. All IEPs must be realistic and progress towards the goals must be measurable.

Integrated services At PPSS, various staff members with different specialities collaborate in order to ensure that relatively scarce resources, such as occupational therapy, physiotherapy and speech therapy, are woven into the curriculum throughout the day. Thus, therapists, teachers and specialists have discussions to agree upon each student's goals, then determine meaningful strategies that can be used throughout the day to achieve these goals. All staff members integrate these practices into every daily routine.

Integrated Services Committee A multidisciplinary group of staff representatives of the various disciplines at the school. The committee meets weekly to discuss and monitor the progress of all students at the school. Students from all classes are systematically reviewed and any staff member or parent can bring any issue to the attention of the committee for discussion and review. The committee can determine what actions need to be taken to support the staff member, student or family.

Intellectual disability (ID) A below-average level of cognitive functioning and associated difficulties with daily living skills (defined by the *Disabilty Act 2006* as 'significant sub-average general intellectual functioning' and 'significant deficits in adaptive behaviour'). To be accepted at a specialist school in the state of Victoria, a student is considered to have an intellectual disability if he or she has a history of delayed or disordered development and has participated in a series of tests, including an IQ test that has resulted in an IQ of 69 or below. More broadly, about three per cent of the general population is considered to have an intellectual disability.

Intensive interaction A style of interaction which attempts to foster communication and sociability in the same way that a caregiver teaches a baby—by playful repetition, modelling and following a child's lead. It is designed to be used with students who have severe disabilities, have autism and are non-verbal. It is based on the theory that everyone needs to communicate even if they cannot speak. It involves doing things on the student's terms and using their non-verbal behaviours as an opportunity to connect with them by modelling what they do.

Key word signing (formerly known as the Makaton Vocabulary) A form of using individual hand signs and gestures to represent people, objects, actions, places and some activities for people who can hear but have difficulty with oral communication. Designed to be used in conjunction with speech, the key words in a sentence are also signed (e.g. in the utterance 'let's sit down' the words 'sit' and 'down' would be signed). It is often used with those who have an intellectual disability to engage attention and encourage communication.

Least restrictive environment The Victorian *Disability Act 2006* (S. 5(4)) states that, 'If a restriction on the rights or opportunities of a person with a disability is necessary, the option chosen should be the option which is the least restrictive of the person as is possible in the circumstances.' In special needs education, this approach is related to inclusive education, and aims to ensure that students with and without disabilities are educated together as much as possible and have equal access to educational programs, environments and opportunities. The approach has been criticised, however, where it results in students with disabilities being 'mainstreamed' rather than provided with fully-serviced schools with specially designed learning programs (see, for example, Autism Victoria 2002; Dixon & Verenikina 2007).

Mainstream classroom ('mainstreaming') The legal policy of allowing and encouraging students with special needs to be enrolled in typical or 'mainstream' classrooms with typically developing peers. Every student with a disability is entitled to attend their local mainstream or regular school. While placing students in a mainstream school is often viewed as the best option for students, in Australia, mainstream schools may not have access to appropriate therapy services to provide additional guidance and support for a student's program.

MightyMo An electronic communication device designed for people who have limited or no speech. The device, which can be customised for an individual user, has digital speech output which can generate some speech-like voices. It can give a person with limited speech capabilities a 'voice'. The MightyMo is an older model; similar products include DynaVox communication devices such as the M3.

Musical Instrument Digital Interface (MIDI) This is a device that uses a digital language that allows music to be encoded, stored, decoded and played back. In terms of students with intellectual disabilities, it allows them to 'play musical instruments' by using a keyboard or touch pad.

Occupational therapy A therapy designed to teach skills needed for the activities we use in daily life. Occupational therapists (OTs) help people to overcome any difficulties they may have in performing various tasks as a result of an intellectual disability or physical disability, age, illness or injury. An OT concentrates on fine motor activities—meaning the smaller muscles in the hands, fingers, toes and mouth. Picking up an object between thumb and forefinger is an example of a fine motor skill. Many OTs today also assist with identifying sensory processing disorders and treatments using sensory diets and sensory menus.

Percutaneous endoscopic gastrostomy tube (PEG) A plastic tube used to provide nutrients to people who cannot take food via their mouth. The tube bypasses the mouth and goes directly to the stomach. Food with specialised nutrients is provided by the doctor or family and staff who do the feeding get specialised training from nursing staff at the Royal Children's Hospital.

Personalised learning This entails using the individual student's interests, strengths or personal learning style. It involves creating a learning program for every student at a school, tracking progress and assisting each student to achieve his or her greatest possible educational outcomes or success.

Physiotherapy A therapy designed to help improve the strength, coordination and abilities of those who have a physical disability or disorder. A physical therapist (or physiotherapist) uses exercises and equipment to help a person acquire or improve gross motor skills such as crawling, walking and running.

Picture Communication Symbols (PCS) These are visual picture symbols used to foster communication. Each picture shows an object, place, action or person. Symbols can be photographs or drawings and may be used with or without text (e.g. a picture of an apple with the word 'apple' written underneath). PPSS uses symbols on five-by-five centimetre laminated squares, usually attached to a board or plastic strip with double-sided tape. They are used to show a daily schedule of events, a timetable or a sequence of steps to complete an activity, or they can be used by a student or teacher to represent an event, activity or choice. Many of the PCS symbols are available via a computer program called Boardmaker®.

Picture Exchange Communication System (PECS) This is a widely used and well-regarded tool for helping students with language difficulties to learn to communicate. PECS can utilise PCS (see above) or actual objects. A student can communicate by exchanging a picture to receive a desired object or activity. At PPSS, the symbolic pictures are used in classrooms throughout the school; all students who do not have the ability to communicate are given extensive practice in using PECS (Hart & Banda 2010; Magiato & Howlin 2003; Sulzer-Azaroff et al. 2009).

Proprioceptors Sensory receptors located in the joints, muscles, tendons and inner ear which sense movement and help a person to identify where he or she is in space. These skills are needed to be able to stand, walk, run and so on.

Resonance board A hollow box which can be used by a person who is deaf or blind or who has an intellectual disability, in order to feel vibrations and to perceive 'sound'.

RiSE Symposium The International Symposium on Re-imagining Special Education through Arts Education and Arts Therapy was held in Melbourne in 2008, hosted by PPSS.

Scaffolding Assisting a student in planning, organising or practising a skill to help the student learn more, and learn more quickly. Ideally, scaffolding expands the zone of proximal development (see below) by giving the student support to use old learning to link to new learning.

Sensory diet A set of activities selected from a sensory menu (see below), tailored specifically for an individual student who has a sensory processing disorder (see below). These activities should help alleviate or meet the sensory requirements for the student.

Sensory menu Activities and associated pieces of equipment for treating sensory processing disorders (see below). Some examples include: brushing the skin with a special brush; use of deep-pressure massage; wearing specially designed weighted vests; using a trampoline or treadmill. These activities should be prescribed by an occupational therapist. They should not be done with every student as they must be individually prescribed. Using them incorrectly or for the wrong individual may be harmful.

Sensory processing The primal and instant response of a human being to information received through one or more of our senses of sight, hearing, touch, taste, smell, balance and proprioception (see above).

Sensory processing disorder The existence of sensory processing disorders is not fully established in the scientific literature; however, occupational therapists and many families recognise their existence. A sensory processing disorder is believed to be a neurological disorder causing difficulties in taking in, processing and responding to sensory information in the environment and from within one's own body. Unlike blindness or deafness, the sensory information can be received; however, the information is often registered, interpreted and processed differently in the brain. The result can be that a person with a sensory processing disorder over- or under-responds to sensory triggers in the environment, has unusual ways of responding or behaving, and finds everyday things harder to do. Individuals may have difficulties with planning and organisation, self-care, work and leisure activities, and it may result in extreme agitation, stress, fear, confusion or avoidance of activities (Kranowitz, 1998; Rogers et al. 2003; Watling et al. 2001). If a student is considered to have the disorder, the occupational therapist would develop an individualised program or a sensory diet (see above) for the student.

Short Break Cafe On-site cafe operated by the students at PPSS as part of a living skills program. The students learn to set tables, set the cafe menu, purchase supplies, prepare the food, seat patrons, take orders, deliver prepared orders, clean tables, total the patron's costs for their meal, collect money, give appropriate change, bank money, monitor how many items they sell, determine what needs to be purchased for the next working day, and decide how profits are to be spent.

Special developmental school (SDS) Traditionally in Victoria, a school for students whose score on a standardised IQ test measures at 50 or below; however, increasingly, there is crossover between specialist schools (see below) and special developmental schools.

Special education Education designed to foster the specific intellectual, emotional and daily living skills requirements of a person who has an intellectual disability.

Special needs A broad term encompassing a host of disabilities, disorders and conditions which includes developmental delay, autism spectrum disorders, mild to severe intellectual disabilities (which may or may not have accompanying medical or physical conditions), as well as behavioural problems, mental illness, food allergies and major or terminal illness.

Specialist school Traditionally in Victoria, a school for students whose score on a standardised IQ test measures between 51 and 69. Called a 'specialist' school because of the range of specialist staff employed. These schools cater to students aged from four years and eight months to eighteen years old.

Specialist staff This term usually denotes a teacher who is a specialist in a given area, as opposed to a general classroom teacher. Examples of specialist staff members are music, art, drama, swimming and physical education teachers. At PPSS, there are numerous such specialists but they also frequently have other specialist skills for teaching of students with additional needs. Often these staff members have skills and experience beyond the basic teaching qualification.

Speech therapy (also known as speech pathology or speech–language pathology) A therapy designed to help a person acquire or improve communication. This may include speech, language, conversational skills or the ability to tell a story, read, write or spell.

Student Support Group (SSG) According to the Victorian state government's Department of Education and Early Childhood Development, the goal of the Student Support Group is to ensure that those who best know and are responsible for a student with special needs work together to plan educational goals and then monitor progress. This group should always include the parents, the teacher and relevant professional staff members who are knowledgeable about the student with special needs (this may include a medical professional, occupational therapist, physiotherapist, psychologist, speech–language pathologist, and so on).

Syndromes Historically syndromes have been identified by a series of features, characteristics, medical conditions and/or behavioural presentations. Many of the syndromes are named after the individuals who identified these features and some were named after the major biological process that is affected, causing the syndrome. Today, more and more syndromes are identified by genetic testing. See Table 3.1 for some types of syndromes.

Therapy Any form of systematic and planned treatment provided by individuals who have appropriate qualifications to diagnose and treat a particular disorder. Appropriate treatment is selected from a range of options to match individual needs and based on research evidence for effectiveness. These days most qualified therapists are required to only use treatments that have a carefully researched evidence-base. This is called evidence-based practice. Most therapists have completed a university-based program of between two and five years of full-time study as training to practise a therapy. (See also: arts therapy, hydrotherapy, occupational therapy, physiotherapy, speech therapy.)

Time Timer A visual, clock-face timer. As time elapses, a red disc gradually disappears until it is gone, advising the student that time is up, so they can cease working or move to another activity. These can be used with or without an audio signal.

Tracking Visually following an object or text with your eyes without moving your head.

Transition class Students with intellectual disabilities between the ages of approximately 15 and 18 years participate in a program to prepare them for life after school. This may include work-related tasks, leisure activities or some form of supervised living. These classes will vary depending on each student's individual needs and abilities.

United Nations Educational, Scientific and Cultural Organisation (UNESCO) UNESCO promotes educational collaboration around the world, with the aim of helping countries provide quality education for all and lifelong learning. UNESCO has played a major role in sponsoring international conferences and statements on the rights of people with a range of disabilities.

Victorian Essential Learning Standards (VELS) This is the curriculum designed by the state of Victoria for all students to follow from Prep to Year 10.

Visual and Performing Arts Curriculum (VPAC) This curriculum is used at PPSS in order to achieve many of the goals outlined in VELS (see above). PPSS uses visual and performing arts to engage and teach students.

Visual schedule A set of pictures (often using PCS or text) that communicates that a series of activities must be undertaken in a particular sequence or specifies the steps of a specific activity. Visual schedules are meant to help students understand and manage the daily events in their lives. Visual schedules may be created using photographs, pictures, written words or objects. Ideally they communicate clear expectations and allow the student a way to predict what needs to be done or what is going to happen, and thus the student can prepare for the new activity (Bopp et al. 2004; Wheeler & Carter 1998). Preparing a student in this way can decrease anxiety and lead to less stress.

Withdrawal A process whereby a therapist or teacher takes a student out of the classroom for a specific amount of time for a specialised therapy program or instruction. This type of treatment does not agree with the international UNESCO requirements for providing an education in the least restrictive environment. Thus, at PPSS most of the treatments are provided in the classroom and the teachers perform most of the 'therapy program' during routine class activities.

Zone of proximal development A theory developed by psychologist Lev Vygotsky (1962). It holds that the zone of proximal development is the difference between what a student can do without help and what she or she can do with help. Vygotsky believed that the best way to teach a student was by focusing on emerging skills and that teaching a student only slightly ahead of his or her present abilities would help the student learn. If the distance between what is known and what is to be learned is too great the student will not learn. In working with students with disabilities, all teachers must know what the zone of proximal development is for each student.

References

Adelman, H.S. (1993). School-linked mental health interventions: Towards mechanisms for service coordination and integration. *Journal of Community Psychology, 21*, 309-319.

Alward, E.H., Richards, T.L. Berninger, V.W., Nagy, W.E., Field, K.M., Grimme, A.C., Richards, A.L., Thomson, J.B., & Cramer, S.C. (2003). Instructional teaching associated with changes in brain activation in children with dyslexia. *Neurology, 61*, 212–219.

Anning, A., Cottrell, D., Frost, N., Green, J., & Robinan, M. (2006). *Developing multidisciplinary teams for integrated children's services.* London: Open University Press.

Autism Victoria (2002). *'Better Services Better Outcomes': Response from Autism Victoria* [letter to the Department of Education, Employment and Training, 18 January 2002]. Retrieved from www.autismvictoria.org.au/policy/AutismPolicy02.pdf

Barber, M. (2008). Using Intensive Interaction to add to the palette of interactive possibilities in teacher–pupil communication. *European Journal of Special Needs Education, 23*(4), 393–402.

Barber, M., & Mourshed, M. (2007). *How the world's best-performing school systems come out on top.* London: McKinsey & Company. Retrieved from www.mckinsey.com/App_Media/Reports/SSO/Worlds_School_Systems_Final.pdf

Berg, K. (2010). Justifying physical education based on neuroscience evidence. *Journal of Physical Education, Recreation and Dance, 81*, 1–60.

Berra, Y., & Kaplan, D. (2002). *What time is it? You mean now? Advice for life from the Zennest of them all.* New York: Simon & Schuster.

Berrol, C.F. (2006). Neurosciences meets dance/movement therapy: Mirror neurons, the therapeutic process and empathy. *The Arts in Psychotherapy, 33*, 302–315.

Blakemore, S-J., & Frith, U. (2005). The learning brain: Lessons for education: A précis. *Developmental Science, 8*, 459–471.

Blood, A.J., Zatorre, R.J., Berudez, P., & Evans, A.C. (1999). Emotional responses to pleasant and unpleasant music correlate with activity in paralimbic brain regions. *Nature Neuroscience, 2*, 382–387.

Bopp, K.D., Brown, K.E., & Mirenda, P. (2004). Speech–language pathologists' roles in the delivery of positive behaviour support for individuals with developmental disabilities. *American Journal of Speech Language Pathology, 13,* 5–19.

Bransford, J., Brown, A., & Cocking, R. (1999). *How people learn: Brain, mind, experience and school.* Washington, DC: National Academy Press.

Brown, S.M.K. (1994). Autism and music therapy: Is change possible and why music? *Journal of British Musical Therapy, 8,* 15–25.

Brown, S., & Parsons, L.M. (2008). The neuroscience of dance. *Scientific American, 299,* 78–83.

Brownwell, M.D. (2002). Musically adapted social stories to modify behaviour in students with autism: Four case studies. *Journal of Music Therapy, 39,* 117–144.

Bruder, M., & Bologna, T. (1993). Collaboration and service coordination for effective early intervention. In W. Brown, S.K. Thurman, & L. Peters (Eds.), *Family-centered early intervention with families and toddlers: Innovative cross-disciplinary approaches* (pp. 103–128). Baltimore: Paul H Brookes.

Buday, E.M. (1995). The effects of signed and spoken words taught with music on sign and speech imitation by children with autism. *Journal of Music Therapy, 32,* 189–202.

Burt, M.R. Resnick, G., & Matheson, N. (1992). *Comprehensive service integration programs for at-risk youth.* Washington, DC: Urban Institute.

Burton, J., Horowitz, R., & Abeles, H. (1999). *Learning in and through the arts: Curriculum implications.* New York: Teachers College Press.

Byrnes, J.P. (2001). *Minds, brains, and education: Understanding the psychological and educational relevance of neuroscience research.* New York: Guilford.

Caldwell, B.J. (2008, 28 February). Finns lead the way in literacy. *The Mercury,* p. 28.

Caldwell, B.J., & Harris, J. (2008). *Why not the best schools?* Melbourne: ACER Press.

Calfee, C., Witter, F., & Meredith, M. (1998). *Building a full-service school: A step-by-step guide.* San Francisco, CA: Jossey-Bass.

Carbo, M., Dunn, R., & Dunn, K. (1986). *Teaching students to read through their individual learning styles.* New York: Prentice-Hall.

Carlsson, I., Wendt, P.E., & Risberg, J. (2000). On the neurobiology of creativity: Differences in frontal activity between high and low creative subjects. *Neuropsychologia, 38,* 873–885.

Chen, J.L., Penhune, V.B., & Zatorre, R.J. (2008). Listening to musical rhythms recruits motor regions of the brain. *Cerebral Cortex, 18,* 2844–2854.

Coufal, K.L. (1993). Collaborative consultation for speech-language pathologists. *Topics in Language Disorders, 14,* 1–14.

Curatolo, P., Porfirio, M.C., Manzi, B., & Seri, S. (2004). Autism in tuberous sclerosis. *European Journal of Paediatric Neurology, 8*(6), 327–332.

Damasio, A. (1994). *Descartes' error. Emotion, reason and the human brain.* New York: Putnam.

Dana Foundation (2005). *Arts and cognition: Progress report on brain research*. New York: Dana Foundation and the Dana Alliance for Brain Initiatives.

Darby, J.T., & Catterall, J.S. (1994). The fourth R: The arts and learning. *Teachers College Record, 96*, 299–328.

Davis, W.B., & Thaut, M.H. (1989). The influence of preferred relaxing music on measures of state anxiety, relaxation, and physiological responses, *Journal of Music Therapy, 26*, 168–187.

Deasy, R.J. (Ed.) (2002). *Critical links: Learning in the arts and student academic and social development*. Washington, DC: Arts Education Partnership. Retrieved from http://aep-arts.org/files/publications/CriticalLinks.pdf

de Bono, E. (1985). *Six thinking hats: An essential approach to business management*. Boston: Little, Brown & Company.

Descartes, R. (1644). *Principles of philosophy*, translated by V.R. Miller & R.P. Miller, 1991, Dordrecht: Kluwer Academic Publishers.

Dettmer, S., Simpson, R.L., Myles, B.S., & Ganz, J.B. (2000). The use of visual supports to facilitate transitions of students with autism. *Focus on Autism and Other Developmental Disabilities, 15*(3), 163–169.

Disability Act 2006 (Victoria). Retrieved from the Victorian Statute Book at www.legislation.vic.gov.au

Dixon, R.M., & Vereninka, I. (2007). Towards inclusive schools: An examination of socio-cultural theory and inclusive practices and policy in New South Wales DET schools. *Learning and Sociocultural Theory: Exploring Modern Vygotskian Perspectives International Workshop 2007, 1*(1), 192–208.

Doidge, N. (2007). *The brain that changes itself: Stories of personal triumph for the frontiers of sciences*. New York: Viking Press.

Draganski, B., Gaser, C., Volker, B., Shuierer, G., Bogdahn, U., & May, A. (2004). Neuroplasticity: Changes in grey matter induced by training. *Nature, 427*, 311–312.

Dryfoos, J.G. (1994). *Full-service schools: A revolution in health and social services for children, youth, and families*. San Fransisco: Jossey-Bass.

Dunbar, K.N. (2008). Arts education, the brain, and language. In C. Asbury, & B. Rich (Eds.), *Learning, arts, and the brain: The Dana Consortium report of the arts and cognition*. New York: Dana Press.

Ehren, B. (2000). Maintaining a therapist's focus and sharing responsibilities for student success: Keys to in-classroom speech-language services. *Language, Speech, Hearing Services in Schools, 31*, 219–229.

Eisner, E.W. (1998). Does experience in the arts boost academic achievement? *Art Education, 51*, 7–15.

Elfand, A.D. (2002). *Art and cognition: Integrating the visual arts in the curriculum*. New York: Teachers College Press.

Ellis, R.D. (1999). The dance for of the eyes: What cognitive science can learn from art. *Journal of Consciousness Studies, 6*, 6–7.

Essex, M., Frostig, K., & Hertz, J. (1996). In the service of children: Art and expressive therapies in public schools. *Art Therapy: Journal of the American Art Therapy Association, 13*, 181–190.

Fogg, T., & Smith, M. (2001). The artists in the classroom project: A closer look. *Educational Forum, 66*, 60–70.

Gallagher, S.A., & Gallagher, J.J. (2002). Giftedness and Asperger's Syndrome: A new agenda for education. *Understanding Our Gifted, 14*(2), 7–12.

Gangwer, T. (2009). *Visual impact, visual teaching: Using images to strengthen learning.* London: Corwin Press.

Gardiner, M.F., Fox, A., Knowles, F., & Jeffery, D. (1996). Learning improved by arts training. *Nature, 381*, 284.

Gardner, H. (1985). *Frames of mind: The theory of multiple intelligences.* New York: Basic Books.

Gardner, H. (1993). *Multiple intelligence: The theory in practice.* New York: Basic Books.

Gardner, H. (1999). *Intelligence reframed: Multiple intelligences for the 21st century.* New York: Basic Books.

Gardner, H. (2006). *Five minds for the future.* Boston: Harvard Business School Press.

Gardner, H., & Hatch, T. (1989). Educational implications of the theory of multiple intelligences. *Educational Researcher, 18*, 4–10.

Garvey, C.J. (1977). *Play.* Cambridge, MA: Harvard University Press.

Giangreco, M.F. (1986). Effects of integrated therapy: A pilot study. *Journal of the Association for Persons with Severe Handicaps, 11*, 205–208.

Giangreco, M.F., Edelman, S., & Dennis, R. (1991). Common professional practices that interfere with the integrated delivery of related services. *Remedial and Special Education, 12*, 151–159.

Giffin, H. (1984). The coordination of meaning in the creation of shared make-believe reality. In I. Bretherton (Ed.), *Symbolic play* (pp. 73–100). San Diego, CA: Academic Press.

Gillard, J. (2008, 18 July). John Button Memorial Lecture. Delivered in Melbourne 17 July 2008. Retrieved from www.theage.com.au/opinion/john-button-memorial-lecture-20080717-3h1n.html

Goodwyn, S.W., Acredolo, L.P., & Brown, C. (2000). Impact of symbolic gesturing on early language development. *Journal of Nonverbal Behaviour, 24*, 81–103.

Greenough, W.T., Black, J.E., & Wallace, C.S. (1987). Experience and brain development. *Child Development, 58*, 539–559.

Grezes, J., Costes, N., & Decety, J. (1999). The effects of learning and intention on the neural network involved in the perception of meaningless actions. *Brain, 122*, 1875–1887.

Grove, N., & Walker, M. (1990). The Makaton vocabulary: Using manual signs and graphic symbols to develop interpersonal communication. *Augmentative and Alternative Communication, 6*, 15–28.

Gullatt, D.E. (2008). Enhancing student learning through arts integration: Implications for the profession. *High School Journal, 91*(4), 12–25.

Hamblen, K.A. (1993). Theories and research that support art instruction for instrumental outcomes. *Theory into Practice, 32*(4), 191–198.

Hart, S.L., & Banda, D.R. (2010). Picture Exchange Communication System with individuals with developmental disabilities: A meta-analysis of single subject studies. *Remedial and Special Education, 31*(6), 476–488.

Hartley, S.L., & Sikora, D.M. (2009). Sex differences in autism spectrum disorders: An examination of developmental functioning, autistic symptoms, and coexisting behaviour problems in toddlers. *Journal of Autism and Developmental Disorders, 39*(12), 1715–1722.

Heath, S.B. & Roach, A. (1999). Imaginative actuality: Learning in the arts during the nonschool hours. In E. Fiske (Ed.), *Champions of change: Impact of the arts on learning.* Washington, DC: The Arts Education Partnership and the President's Committee on the Arts and Humanities.

Howes, C. (1985). Sharing fantasy: Social pretend play in toddlers. *Child Development, 56*, 1253–1258.

Howes, C., Unger, O.A., & Seidner, L.B. (1989). Social pretend play in toddlers: Parallels with social play and with solidarity pretend. *Child Development, 60*, 77-84.

Iacono, T., & Johnson, H. (2004). Patients with disabilities and complex communication needs: The GP consultation. *Australian Family Physician, 33*, 585–589.

Ivey, A.E., Ivey, M.B., & Simek-Downing, L. (1987). *Counselling and Psychotherapy: Integrating skills, theory and practice* (pp. 78–79), Prentice-Hall International: New Jersey.

Jellison, J., Brooks, B., & Huck, A. (1984). Strucuring small groups and music reinforcement to facilitate positive interactions and acceptance of handicapped students in the regular music class. *Journal of Research in Music Education, 32*, 243–264.

Jensen, E. (2001). *Arts with the brain in mind.* Alexandria: Association for Supervision and Curriculum Development.

Johnson, P. (2006). *Creators.* New York: Harper Perennial.

Johnson, S., Nelson, C., Evans, J., & Palazolo, K. (2003). The use of visual supports in teaching young children with autism spectrum disorders to initiate interactions. *Augmentative and Alternative Communication, 19*(2), 86–103.

Jones, P. (2005). *The arts therapies: A revolution in healthcare.* Hove, East Sussex: Brunner-Routledge.

Kaczmarek, L., Pennington, R., & Goldstein, H. (2000). Transdisciplinary consultation: A center-based team functioning model. *Education and Treatment of Children, 23*, 156–172.

Katagiri, J. (2009). The effect of background music and song texts on the emotional understanding of children with autism. *Journal of Music Therapy, 46*, 15–31.

Kellett, M. (2004). Intensive interaction in the inclusive classroom: Using interactive pedagogy to connect with students who are hardest to reach. *Westminster Studies in Education, 27*, 175–188.

Kemmis, B.L., & Dunn, W. (1996). Collaborative consultation: The efficacy of remedial and compensatory interventions in school contexts. *American Journal of Occupational Therapy, 50*, 709–717.

King, G.A., McDougall, J., Tucker, M.A., Gritzan, J., Malloy-Miller, T., Alambets, P., Cunning, D., Thomas, K., & Gregory, K. (2000). An evaluation of functional, school-based therapy services for children with special needs. *Physical and Occupational Therapy in Pediatrics, 19*(2), 5–29.

Kowatari, Y., Lee, S.H., Yamamara, H., Nagamori, Y., Levy, P., Yamane, S., & Yamamoto, M. (2009). Neural networks involved in artistic creativity. *Human Brain Mapping, 30*, 1678–1690.

Kranowitz, C.S. (1998). *The Out-of-sync child: Recognizing and coping with sensory integration dysfunction.* New York: The Berkley Publishing Group.

MacDermott, S., Williams, K., Ridley, G., Glasson, E., & Wray, J. (2007). *The prevalence of autism in Australia: Can it be established from existing data?* Frenchs Forest, NSW: Australian Advisory Board on Autism Spectrum Disorders. Retrieved from www.autismaus.com.au/uploads/pdfs/PrevalenceReport.pdf

McEwen, B.S. (2000a). Allostasis and allostatic load: Implications for neuropsychopharmacology. *Neuropsychopharmacology, 22*, 108–124.

McEwen, B.S. (2000b). Effects of adverse experiences for brain structure and function. *Biological Psychiatry, 48*, 721–731.

McEwen, B.S. (2000c). Protective and damaging effects of stress mediators: Central role of the brain. In E.A. Mayer, & C.B. Saper (Eds.), *Progress in brain research, Vol. 122: The biological basis for mind body* interactions (pp. 25–34). Amsterdam: Elsevier.

McMahon, S.D., Rose, D.S., & Parks, M. (2003). Basic reading through dance program: The impact on first-grade students' basic reading skills. *Evaluation Review, 27*, 104–125.

McWilliam, R.A. (1995). Integration of therapy and consultative special education: A continuum in early intervention. *Infants and Young Children, 7*, 29–38.

McWilliam, R.A., & Scott, S. (2003). *Integrating therapy into the classroom: The national individualizing preschool inclusion project.* Washington, DC:

US Department of Education, Office of Special Education Programs. Retrieved from www.nectac.org/~pdfs/Meetings/InclusionMtg2005/ IntegratedServices-Ap2005.pdf

McWilliam, R.A., & Sekerak, D. (1995). Integrated practices in centre-based early intervention: Perceptions of physical therapists. *Pediatric Physical Therapy*, 7, 51–58.

Magiati, I., & Howlin, P. (2003). A pilot evaluation study of the Picture Exchange Communication System (PECS) for children with autistic spectrum disorders. *Autism*, 7, 297–320.

Mason, C., Thormann, M., & Steedly, K. (2004). *How students with disabilities learn in and through the arts: An investigation of educator perceptions.* Washington DC: A VSA Affiliate Research Project. Retrieved from www.kennedy-center.org/ education/vsa/resources/arpfinaldraft.pdf

Moreno, S., Marques, C., Santos, A., Santos, M., Castro, S.L., & Besson, M. (2009). Musical training influences linguistic abilities in 8-year-old children: More evidence for brain plasticity. *Cerebral Cortex*, 19, 712–723.

National Curriculum Board (Australia) (2008, June). *National Curriculum Development Paper.* Presented at the National Curriculum Board Forum, Melbourne. Retrieved from www.acara.edu.au/verve/_resources/ development_paper.pdf

Parsons, C. (2007). Integrated services. *Port Phillip Specialist School Yearbook*, p. 18.

Parsons, C. (2010). Integrated services are the heartbeat of the school. *Port Phillip Specialist School Yearbook*, p. 14.

Pasiali, V. (2004). The use of prescriptive therapeutic songs in a home-based environment to promote social skills acquisition by children with autism: Three case studies. *Music Therapy Perspectives*, 22, 11–20.

Phillips, L., Sapona, R.H., & Lubic, B.C. (1995). Developing partnerships in inclusive education. *Intervention in Schools and Clinic*, 30, 262–272.

Port Phillip Specialist School (no date). *Education through the arts.* Melbourne: Port Phillip Specialist School.

Posner, M., Rothbart, M.K., Sheese, B.E., & Kieras, J. (2008). How arts training influences cognition. In C. Asbury, & B. Rich (Eds.), *Learning, arts, and the brain: The Dana Consortium report of the arts and cognition.* New York: Dana Press.

Prigge, D. (2002). Promote brain-based teaching and learning. *Intervention in School and Clinic*, 37, 237–241.

Pring, L., Hermelin, B., Buhler, M., & Walker, I. (1997). Native savant talent and acquired skill. *Autism*, 1, 199–214.

Reiter, M. (2002, 2003). *Magic 100 Words.* Melbourne: Magic Words International.

Riccio, L., Rollins, J., & Morton, K. (2003). *The SAIL effect: Development of a model for measuring the effectiveness of the arts as an instrumental element in overall academic and social development for students in an art-infused elementary school.* Washington, DC: VSA Connection.

Rogers, C.R. (1967). Interpersonal relationship: The core of guidance. In C.R. Rogers, & B. Stevens, *Person to person: The problem of being human.* Lafayette, CA: Real People Press.

Rogers, S.J, Hepburn, S., & Wehner, E. (2003). Parent reports of sensory symptoms in toddlers with autism and those with other developmental disorders. *Journal of Autism & Developmental Disorders, 33,* 631–642.

Rose, G.J. (2004). *Between couch and piano: Psychoanalysis, music, art and neuroscience.* New York: Brunner-Routledge.

Ruppert, S.S. (2006). *Critical evidence: How the arts benefit student achievement.* Washington, DC: National Assembly of State Arts Agencies and Arts Education Partnership.

Rutter, M. (2005). Incidence of autism spectrum disorders: Changes over time and their meaning. *Acta Paediatrica, 94*(1), 2–15.

Sacks, O. (2007). *Musicophilia: Tales of Music and the Brain.* London: Picador.

Samuel, J., Nind, M., Volans, A., & Scriven, I. (2008). An evaluation of intensive interaction in community living settings for adults with profound intellectual disabilities. *Journal of Intellectual Disabilities, 12,* 111–126.

Schwartz, I.S., Carta, J.J., & Grant, S. (1996). Examining the use of recommended language intervention practices in early childhood special education classrooms. *Topics in Early Childhood Special Education, 16,* 251–272.

Spelke, E. (2008). Effects of music instruction on developing cognitive systems at the foundations of mathematics and science. In C. Asbury and B. Rich (Eds.), *Learning, arts, and the brain: The Dana Consortium report of the arts and cognition.* New York: Dana Press.

Spencer, S.A. (2005). The practicalities of collaboration and special education service delivery. *Intervention in School and Clinic, 40,* 296–300.

Stafford, R., & Dunn, K.J. (1993). *Teaching secondary students through their individual learning styles.* New York: Allyn and Bacon.

Sulzer-Azaroff, B., Hoffman, A.O., Horton, C.B., Bondy, A., & Frost, L. (2009). The Picture Exchange Communication system (PECS): What do the data say? *Focus on Autism and Other Developmental Disabilities, 24,* 89–103.

Torrance, J. (2003). Autism, aggression, and developing a therapeutic contract. *American Journal of Dance Therapy, 25,* 97–109.

Vygotsky, L.S. (1962). *The development of scientific concepts in childhood: Thought and language.* Cambridge, MA: MIT Press.

Walker, J. (2008, 5 March). Seems I'll have to eat my hat. *The Mercury,* p. 32.

Wallace, G.L., Happe, F., & Giedd, J.N. (2009). A case study of a multiply talented savant with an autism spectrum disorder: Neurophysiological functioning and brain morphometry. *Philosophical Transactions of the Royal Society of Biological Sciences, 364,* 1425–1432.

Warger, C. (2001). *Research on full-service schools and students with disabilities* (ERIC/OSEP Digest ED458749). Arlington, VA: ERIC Clearinghouse on Disabilities and Gifted Education. Retrieved from www.eric.ed.gov/PDFS/ED458749.pdf

Watling, R.I., Deitz, J., & White, O. (2001). Comparison of sensory profile scores of young children with and without autism spectrum disorders. *American Journal of Occupational Therapy, 55,* 416–423.

Watson, J., & Knight, C. (1991). An evaluation of intensive interactive teaching with pupils with very severe learning difficulties. *Child Language Teaching and Therapy, 7,* 310–325.

Weiner, I., & Murawski, W.W. (2005). Schools attunded: A model for collaborative intervention. *Intervention in School and Clinic, 40,* 284–290.

Wellcome Trust Sanger Institute (2009, 19 April). *The genetic X-factor: Nine new chromosome genes associated with learning disabilities* [Media release]. Retrieved from www.sanger.ac.uk/about/press/2009/090419.html

Wheeler, J.J., & Carter, S.L. (1998). Using visual cues in the classroom for learners with autism as a method for promoting positive behaviour. *Journal of Special Education, 21,* 64–73.

Whitmire, K. (2002). The evolution of school-based speech-language services: A half century of change and a new century of practice. *Communication Disorders Quarterly, 23,* 68–76.

Winner, E., & Hetland, L. (2000). The arts and academic achievement: What the evidence shows. Executive Summary. *The Journal of Aesthetic Education, 34,* 3–4.

York, J., Rainforth, B., & Giangreco, M.F. (1990). Transdisciplinary teamwork and integrated therapy: Clarifying the misconceptions. *Pediatric Physical Therapy, 2,* 73–79.

Zaidel, D.W. (2010). Art and brain: Insights from neuropsychology, biology and evolution. *Journal of Anatomy, 216,* 177–183.

Zimmerman, E. (1997). Excellence and equity issues in art education: Can we be excellent and equal too? *Arts Education Policy Review, 98,* 20–26.

The Australian Council *for* Educational Research,
SAVAGE Films, The Pratt Foundation,
The Business Working with Education Foundation,
the Victorian Department of Education and
Early Childhood Development,
and The Ian Potter Foundation

present …

'Dare to be different'

An education documentary about an extraordinary school.

'Dare to be different' is the extraordinary story of Port Phillip Specialist School which, under the leadership of former principal Bella Irlicht, evolved from a one-room facility to a world-class, fully serviced education environment with a unique arts-based curriculum that powerfully impacts the lives of its special needs students and their families.

At the time of going to print, the documentary is in production at the school. It is a companion piece to the book *An Extraordinary School* and will be completed in March 2013.

CONTACT
Producer: Annemarie Rolls
03 8660 5103
annemarie.rolls@bwefoundation.org.au